SATAN-PROOF YOUR CHILDREN

*Red alert signals for parents
with children in school*

SATAN-PROOF
Your
CHILDREN

Red alert signals for parents
with children in school

GRACE AKANLE

EMMANUEL HOUSE
London, United Kingdom

Satan-Proof Your Children
Copyright ©1999 by Grace Akanle

Published by
Emmanuel House
PO Box 15022
London
SE5 7ZL

All Scriptures, unless otherwise stated, are taken from the *King James Version* of the Bible.

Scriptures marked GNB are taken from the *Good News Bible* published by The Bible Society, 1966, 1971, 1976, 1992.

ISBN 1 900529 06 8

Cover design by *HimPressions*
Printed in England by Cox & Wyman Ltd.,
Reading, Berkshire

CONTENTS

ACKNOWLEDGEMENTS

NOTHING JUST happens. The book you are about to read is not an accident but a timely exposition that God intended for this season. I thank my God, therefore, who chose, prepared, prompted and empowered me to put this book together.

The urge to write *Satan-Proof Your Children* came after attending a seminar organised by the *International Ministerial Council of Great Britain (IMCGB)*. I thank God for the concern they have for children's welfare and education.

I thank Pastor Tokunbo Emmanuel and his wife, Linda, of *Emmanuel House*, for being a motivation for me throughout the writing of this book and their input in its production.

I thank Pastors Tayo and Lola Oyebade for their prayers and support. Pastors David and Sola Goriola have also been a great support to me and my family. I sincerely thank Mrs. Eniola Dipeolu for being a friend in need and a friend indeed. Thanks to Evangelist Grace Adejuwon for her encouragement and to Bishop Titus 'Gbenga David for kindly writing the foreword.

I am grateful to God for my godly children, Christina, Clementine and Stephanie for their patience, comfort, moral support and constant prayers for *mummy*.

Finally, I appreciate the Lord of Hosts who purposes a thing and brings it to pass. He deserves all the praise. Father, it is a privilege to serve you!

- Rev. Grace Akanle
Secretary, IMCGB Southwark & Lambeth, London

To God's Properties:
Christina,
Clementine
and
Stephanie.
I love you all...

And

To the baby I named Paul.
I love you,
but Jesus loves you more.
(Rest in Peace)

FOREWORD

By Bishop Titus 'Gbenga David

T HE FIRST time I met the Reverend Grace Akanle was at an IMCGB Ministers' Conference, where she spoke forcefully, eloquently, revealingly and convincingly about the challenges facing Christian parents who are concerned about safe and good education for their children in the UK. Some of the facts she brought to light that day were as arresting and shocking, as they were eye-opening. I am delighted that she has now explained and published them in this book.

Children are the future of the society and the Church. Satan, the enemy of God and of His people, will stop at nothing in his bid to *steal, kill* and *destroy*. One of the most significant places he can gain access to our children is the school, where the opportunities and avenues open to him are many and varied. Our children need protection and we cannot afford to be unaware of the enemy's devices.

Satan-Proof Your Children competently shows us why and how to do this. Because I have observed the author to be a practitioner of what she has advanced in this book with her own children, I heartily commend *Satan-Proof Your Children* to every parent, whether Christian or not. Anyone who has anything to do with children needs a copy of this book.

Well done, Reverend Grace! Happy reading, one and all!

Bishop Titus 'Gbenga David
London, UK.

INTRODUCTION

"Train up a child in the way he should go: and when he is old, he will not depart from it" (Proverbs 22:6).

T HE KNOWLEDGE we impart to children is very important. Each concept, suggestion, idea and skill they are exposed to is like a brick that builds up the child and ultimately affects development to adulthood.

In the early years, children are very receptive. They are inquisitive, flexible, perceptive, sensitive, alert, bright and very keen. They learn new things quite easily.

It then means that if you teach a child the way of the world, the child is likely to follow the fashion, language and standards of the world.

On the other hand, if you teach a child the way of the *Word* (the will and commandments of God), the child will not depart from it. He or she is more likely to stick to the path of righteousness that you introduced him or her to early in life.

> *"But continue thou in the things which thou hast learned and hast been assured of, knowing of whom thou hast learned them; **And that from a child thou hast known the holy Scriptures**, which are able to make thee wise unto salvation through faith which is in Christ Jesus" (2 Timothy 3:14,15).*

WHAT ARE CHILDREN LIKE?

As a parent, you need to understand the life of children and how they operate. Even though we have all been children before, we unconsciously expect our kids to think and act as adults.

*Children are like **blank videotapes***; whatever you "record" on them stays with them and will subsequently be played back in life. For instance, if a lot of foul language is used around a child, he or she will definitely use foul language when communicating with others.

Again, *children are like **video recorders*** permanently on "record mode". They are busy "recording" everything that goes on in their environment. After a while, they will try to imitate most, if not all, of what they have "recorded". This is why children like to follow the latest fashion, prefer a kind of music, express themselves with particular slangs, etc.

*Children can also be likened to **a field**.* As parents,

we must be aware of the "seeds" that are planted in our children. The "sowers", too, are as important as the "seeds". There are many "sowers" in the world - people who partake in the development of your child - starting from you, the parent, relatives and friends, the childminder, teachers at school and behind the scenes, the devil. It will take a lot of vigilance on your part to scrutinize the "seeds" sown into your child's life. A lot of "weeding" will also be necessary on a regular basis.

WHERE DO WE FIT IN AS PARENTS?

God has given **you** the responsibility of training your children. In which direction are you rowing the boat of their lives? How closely are you monitoring the different stages of their growth? Do you know the people who are taking part in the moral, spiritual, emotional and physical development of your children? How *well* do we know them?

Have you wondered what happens to your little ones when you are not there? A common expression I find among parents is: "I didn't raise him to be rude! I raised him to respect people! *I don't know where he got that from!*"

The simple truth is that you are not the only one raising your children. The society plays an active role in a variety of ways - through formal education, the media, television, music, videos, fashion, language etc. As the parent, however, you have the ultimate responsibility of raising your children.

God has entrusted into our care these young spirit beings we call children. They belong to God, but He has given us the duty of watching over them in this life. We are their caretakers and we are answerable to God. We will all account for the part and role we play in the development of each of the kids God blesses us with.

Knowing this, we need to prayerfully nurture our children and direct them in the right path. They need "balanced diets" of the Bread of life constantly, not the junk food of worldly things, to keep them from suffering moral, emotional and spiritual malnutrition. This is why *Satan-Proof Your Children* has been written.

OBJECTIVES

The aim of this book is to expose the diverse tactics Satan is employing to lure children to his kingdom, thus helping parents to target prayers to specific areas of concern. The book will help you re-structure your strategies of overseeing your children's development. It will increase your sensitivity to their needs and help you to know when they are in need of encouragement, discipline, instruction and affirmation.

This book is not written to criticise schools or the educational system. Neither is it written to teach you how to be a parent (only God can do this). Its objective is to give you an insight into what goes on in the four walls of your child's school. It is written to stimulate your awareness of the strategic and systematic ways the devil is infiltrating into the educational market and the disguise he is using to carry out his dirty tricks.

This book will inform you of the people who participate in your children's learning, the type of programme designed for teaching them and what materials and equipment are used in the learning process. You will realise, sadly, that a lot of what goes on in (and out) of school is detrimental to the moral and spiritual growth of your children.

After reading this book, my prayer and expectation is that the Church will boldly rise up and stop Satan in his tracks; that parents and pastors alike will develop a vision of a better future for our children. Parents, it is time to *Satan-Proof Your Children!*

SECTION ONE:

THE BASICS

The School Environment

The School Workers

The Schoolmates

CHAPTER ONE

THE SCHOOL ENVIRONMENT

A SCHOOL FOR THE COMMUNITY

A SCHOOL is primarily created for its immediate environment. If you survey the population of children in a particular school, you will find out that 75% of the children in that school live around the school neighbourhood. Consequently, it is the children of that community that your child will come in contact and mingle with.

If the majority of children who live in your community are unruly and out of control, then the schools that serve your community will contain a lot of children of the same character. Your children that attend any of these schools will have to learn together with these children in the same school environment.

Now, since you cannot isolate your children from others when they are in school, unavoidably, your children will get involved with different kinds of children. They will work together in class, be in the school assembly together, play on the school playground, eat in the same dinner hall etc. This is what happens seven hours a day, Monday to Friday of every week that your child goes to school.

YOUR DUTY

You cannot keep your children from going to school because of the fear of ungodly influence. This is a crime that can warrant an arrest. Your children are fully entitled to the education the country has to offer. However, when you register your children in a school, it is your duty to find out all you can about the environment in which the school is situated. This will enable you to pray fervently and intelligently for the community's spiritual atmosphere; that it may suit your child's development in line with God's Word and standards.

Wherever the soles of our feet touch, God promised, will be given unto us as an inheritance. The soles of your child's feet will be touching that school environment everyday, so the atmosphere of that area must be subdued.

Different communities are known for different traits. Through prayer you can turn the negative "label" attached to an environment around for the better. For the sake of your children, this is crucial. Your intercession will benefit your children and others that learn together with them.

The principality ruling your child's school environment must be evicted through prayer. Let the devil know that he has no right or power over your children. A line has been drawn with the precious blood of Jesus Christ, over which he must not cross. Do not stand by and watch your children become a victim of their school environment.

CHAPTER TWO

THE SCHOOL WORKERS

D IFFERENT PEOPLE work with your children everyday, discharging one duty or the other. They relate with your children directly or indirectly, and have a level of influence over their life in school. It is important for parents to know the academic set-up of schools and the people who contribute significantly to their children's development.

The category of people who work with your children are as follows:

1. Teaching Staff

2. Administrative staff

3. School helpers (employed)

4. Voluntary workers

5. Governing body

TEACHING STAFF

The teaching staff includes the **headteacher** who oversees the day to day running of the school. The headteacher also attends to the general official issues that involve the school.

Next to the headteacher are the **classroom teachers**. There are different categories of classroom teachers. First, there are the **full-time/permanent teaching staff** who have responsibility for respective classrooms and who are in charge of planning, delivering, reviewing, assessing and keeping records of the children's learning.

Then, there are the **supply teachers** who work for various teaching agencies and are called upon when needed to cover for teachers who are off sick, on maternity or study leave, etc. Supply teachers may work in a school on a one-day contract, a couple of days, a week or for a whole term, depending on the need of the school.

There is also a group of teachers called **section eleven teachers**. These are teachers who teach a special group of children called commonwealth children, who have English as a second language (bilingual children). These teachers work in different classes alongside the classroom teachers. They either work with their special group of children within the main class or take them into a separate room outside the class.

ADMINISTRATIVE STAFF

The next category of workers in a school are the people responsible for taking care of the school's paper-work and the people who attend to other day-to-day issues in the school.

These include the **school secretary**. This school worker sorts out admissions, types out letters, collates the attendance registers with the dinner registers, and does a host of other things in the school office. The secretary is the one you book appointments with to see the headteacher. Nowadays, they prefer to be called administrative officers.

The **school keeper** lives in the compound or around the school premises as a **Caretaker**, the **school nurse** visits the school from time to time, and the **Kitchen staff** work together with the **dinner ladies** to organise the children's school dinner.

SCHOOL HELPERS

School helpers are employed to help a group of children within the classroom set up. These class helpers are also called **school-teaching assistants' (STA)**. Their job is to work with children who have Special Educational Needs (SEN). The SEN children are so categorised because they may be slow in learning; have behavioural problems or one form of disability or the other (see chapter 11 for more details about SEN).

The STA work alongside teachers in the classroom. When a child is really disruptive to the whole class, the class helper will take the child out for sometime to calm him or her down. We call this "timeout". The child will be brought back into the class after a while - when he or she is ready to conform to classroom regulations.

VOLUNTARY WORKERS

Parents are the major **voluntary workers** you will find coming into the school to help with one thing or the other. They sometimes volunteer to read to a group of children or vice versa. They may assist the class teacher by accompanying the children to swimming lessons. Parents also come on school trips to farms, museums or other places of interest.

GOVERNORS

The governors only come once in a while to see how the school is getting on and to ensure that everything is in place. They also have meetings with school authorities to review policies. They visit classrooms, look at the display of children's work on the wall, talk to the teachers and also talk to the children about their work.

WHY ALL THIS INFOMATION?

These among others, are people your children see, talk to and have one form of contact or another with everyday of school life. But why do you, as a parent, need to know all this?

First of all, among these people there are atheists, alcoholics, gays, Satanists, people of other religious beliefs and a handful of born again Christians (very few, I must say). These different types of people will relate with your children in various ways and at different times. They will all have a level of influence over the children under their care.

While I do not intend to scare anyone with the information I present, the truth still needs to be re-vealed. God's people perish for a lack of knowledge, the Bible says. We have been told not to be ignorant of the devil's devices. Would you be surprised if I tell you that the devil is actively seeking and employing ways to get at your children in school? Many of the instruments he uses, sadly, are the people who teach and work with children - directly or indirectly. A lot of intimidation, manipulation and at times, "witchcraft operation" goes on subtly in the four walls of a school.

AGENTS IN DISGUISE?

Satan is determined to destroy. He is not the fork-tailed, red-cloaked, horned-creature he wants us to think he is. In our day and age, he wears a Rolex wrist watch, designer clothing and is on the fast lane of technological inventions. He has many sites on the internet and massive satellite stations installed in space. If you happen to meet him person to person, your first impression may be, "wow, what a success-ful businessman!"

The enemy we are up against is a master con-man. He is the master of disguise. *"Well, no wonder!* **Even Satan can disguise himself to look like an angel of light!"** *(2 Corinthians 11:14 GNB)*. He means business and will do anything for profits.

In order to influence children early in life, the devil has recruited a lot of "agents" into the education market. He has stationed people in every department of education, especially teaching.

Some "agents" desperately work their way into high positions and form a band of the management team in many schools. Sadly, they are the ones who cluster together to make decisions and policies about your children's educational development.

"I CAN'T STAND CHILDREN!"

I have heard quite a number of teachers voice out their indignation about the children they teach. Some have blatantly expressed their hatred for children in general. These remarks are frequent and are not just one-off comments.

One headteacher made a statement in my hearing: "I can't stand children", she said. I wondered why she spent her time in a job she did not like. Another teacher said that he could not stand "clever" children and that he hated them with all his being. The reason? Because they ask too many questions and show off their knowledge (obviously too challenging for him!).

While good teachers contribute to the growth of our children, those with dubious agendas have little or no good thing to add to their lives.

AVENUES OF CONTACT

Teachers (both the godly and the ungodly) make contact with your children in a variety of ways. As a parent, you should be aware of these details so that the prayers you say for your children may be well targetted. These "contact points" include:

1. Conversation

2. Eye contact

3. Physical contact

Conversation: A lot of conversation goes on in school, between teacher and pupils, amongst the children themselves etc. Discussions are normal during class teaching sessions, especially during group work.

Now, what a teacher (or other adults) say to children in school is of utmost importance, because teachers have authority over children in the area of their education. Moreover, a teacher's authority over a child is mainly exercised through the teaching, instructions and words communicated to the child.

Examples of conversations that can transpire between a child and a teacher during the cause of a school day are as follows:

Child: "Miss, I've got a headache"

Teacher: "Oh! *You poor thing*, sit down somewhere and have a rest for a while."

Child: "I do not understand this work?"

Teacher: "How many times do I have to explain this task to you? You do not understand because you hardly listen in class. You are too playful! *What are you? A moron? You are not going to go far, are you?*"

In some circumstances, a teacher or other staff, when speaking to a child, may use words like: "Stupid", "Speak of the devil", "You little devil", or "where the hell have you been? "Oh! You are a nasty piece of work." These phrases are pronounced as a joke, out of anger or on impulse.

TURN THE NEGATIVES TO POSITIVE!

It is crucial for you to spend a moment or two praying over your children, cancelling every negative word that may have been pronounced over them consciously or unconsciously. You do not want your child to grow up believing that he or she is stupid and will not amount to anything, do you?

You can stand upon the word of God and speak

positively into their lives.

> *"No weapon formed against you shall prosper;* ***and*** ***every tongue that shall rise against thee in*** ***judgement thou shalt condemn,*** *this is the heritage of the servants of the Lord and their righteousness is of me, saith the Lord"* *(Isaiah 54:17).*

Parents, we must arise and stand on the word and promises of God for our children. The power of life and death is in the mouth; let us speak the word of life into our children.

Whatever negative confession anyone has made concerning your children, turn it around through prayer. Pray that God will turn curses into blessings, scars into stars, failures into favours in Jesus name.

Eye Contact: Another way in which teachers make contact with children in school is through eye contact. This is very important to teachers as they believe that a child is not listening if he or she does not look at the teacher in the eye.

An intimidating look in the face of a child can shatter the child's self-confidence. Some children cannot look straight into the faces of others because of fear or shame. Help your children to build confidence in God and themselves so that negative effects of eye contacts will not affect them.

Physical Contact: Physical contact is made with your child quite often. Teachers touch children at different times. For instance, a tap on the head may be a teacher's way of getting the child's attention.

We must remember our children in school and pray against any transfer of a contrary spirit through "the laying of hands" of others. These seemingly harmless issues should not be taken lightly.

I pray that by the end of this book, you would have gathered enough energy to put together shotgun prayer points that will disband all networks of evil in every area of your children's development.

CHAPTER THREE

THE SCHOOLMATES

ASSOCIATION

W E LIVE in a multicultural and multiracial society. In every school, you will definitely find children from cultures different from yours; children with different backgrounds, attitudes, behaviours, religions and characters.

Some will learn in the same classroom with your children. These are the first set of kids your child will meet and know. The children in other classes will get to know your child on the playground, in the dinner hall, at home time etc.

Some of these children will become friendly with your child, while some will register their dislike for a variety of reasons.

So, how does your children cope with these different people? How do they relate with friends and "foes" alike? Unlike adults, children love to play together without malice, suspicion or caution. If they disagree or quarrel one minute, you will find them inseparable the next. They are innocent, as Adam and Eve were before they sinned in Eden - naked and not ashamed.

"GUESS WHAT?"

Children learn more from their peer groups than they do from the class. I watch them a lot in the class and on the playground. From my observation, I have learnt that children enjoy sharing information they are excited about with one another. They cannot wait to pass it around the class. No matter how irrelevant it is to their class work, they would still whisper about it to somebody else.

It could start with a simple, "Guess what?". One child may say to another, "My Nan is getting a cat to-morrow" or "I will be going to Macdonalds for my next birthday; my mum promised". To adults, such conversations are unnecessary and irrelevant, but to children, it is vital information that somebody else must know about.

During conversations between children, a lot of ideas are pumped into the mind of a Christian child. The things you disallow your child to do or say for spiritual reasons, may be the very things another kid shows off about in school!

AN ILLUSTRATION

For instance, you may have educated your child about the spiritual implications of watching *some* cartoons on television (read more about cartoons on page 61). However, this could be the same programme another child in school is raving and ranting about.

It might start simply with a question, "Did you watch the *Cult* cartoon last night? Ba! It was wicked! It was on at twelve midnight and I enjoyed every bit of it". Your child will then probably say, "I go to bed at nine o'clock and my mum does not allow me to watch *that* cartoon - and this one and that one".

The other child will reply by saying "What? I can't believe your mum doesn't let you watch cartoons! How boring. That's stupid boy! My mum lets me. And I can't believe she sends you to bed at 9 o'clock! My mum lets me stay up as long as I like. What are you then? A baby, ha ha ha!"

After sowing these seeds of rebellion into your child, he then calls other children to come and partake in making fun of your child. The peer pressure starts to build up.

When the other children in class (or in school!) learn about your child's no-cartoon-go-to-bed-at-9 predicament, the effects can be adverse. Afterwards, your child would begin to think, *"If it is okay for Alan, why is it not okay for me? If Jan's mum allows her to stay up late at night, why does mummy send me to bed at 9?"*

Your child will continue to ponder on this even though you have told him reasons why he is not allowed the indulgence.

A RIGHT TO BE DIFFERENT

The above illustrates how innocent children are encouraged to rebel, lie and disobey their parents. They will yield to peer pressure in order to please and conform to the other children in the school.

Children do not want to be the odd one out. They do not yet understand that it is perfectly alright to be different from others, and that its when you are different that you can make a difference.

It is our responsibility as parents to affirm the uniqueness of our children. We need to let them know that God has made them different from others; that they are fearfully and wonderfully made. Our children have a right to be different from others without being ashamed.

Enlighten your children about how to cope with pressure from peers. Teach them to have a mind of their own - the mind of Christ. They need not be carried here and there by the opinions of others. Let them know that what is good for one child, may be dangerous for another. They need to know that as young soldiers of Christ, they must not allow their sacred temple to be defiled by the filth this world has to offer.

BULLYING

I mentioned earlier that within the educational environment, you can find the subtle operation of "witchcraft". You might have been surprised. By definition, *witchcraft* simply is a spirit of influence, manipulation and control. Do not be amazed that this goes on in schools all the time. One of such "witchcraft" practises can be seen among children. It is known by another term, namely, "bullying".

Bullying is the exertion of influence over others by intimidation and violence. In school, bullies exercise control over other children, using the same means. They subdue and enforce their standards over others. They delight in reducing other children to nothing. Through their continuous actions, they gradually take the dignity, confidence, self-esteem of another child away. Ultimately, they crush their victim's spirit through constant torment and oppression.

CHARACTERISTICS OF BULLIES

Bullies are aggressive and bold. They violate human rights by taking liberties and exercising unauthorised control over their chosen victims.

Just as the Pharisees persecuted our Lord Jesus Christ without a cause, bullies torment innocent children for no apparent reason.

Bullies are children with low self-esteem. They are mostly children who suffer from emotional, mental or psychological problems. Their problem makes them insecure, and they attempt to overcome this by dominating others.

Bullies may even be children from comfortable homes, but who just happen to be used by the devil in this area. Even though bullies are insecure, within themselves, they wear a bold face and a tough outlook - like masks - to hide their inner weaknesses. They love to oppress other children, especially the quiet ones.

Bullies do not operate alone; they usually have accomplices. Children who are weak and do not have a mind of their own, are used to help the bully carry out his operations. In this way, they operate in a gang-like fashion.

A bully can be a boy or a girl. Whatever the gender, bullies are nasty in their operation and they hardly show any remorse. If any of your children is suffering in a web of bullies, God will deliver him or her in Jesus name.

Bullies use threats a lot. They command their victims not to say a word to anyone about what goes on between them. I sometimes shiver to my spine when I imagine what an innocent child suffers in silence because of bullies, having been sworn into secrecy by the bully's threats. "If you tell your mum, teacher or anyone, you are dead!".

Other threats used by bullies go like this: "I will call my friends and we will beat you up"; "I will make sure you don't have any friends in this school again"; "I will set you up and get you into big trouble", etc.

Bullies place impossible demands on their victims. For example, the bully may say, "I want money". If the victim says he does not have any, the bully will reply angrily, "Get your mum to give it to you or steal it!".

Dear parent, we have seen a lot of this in schools; it is not a pleasant experience for any child to suffer in the hand of a bully. The devastating effects can last a long time in the mind and heart of the child.

WHAT ARE THE SIGNS TO LOOK FOR IF YOUR CHILD IS BEING BULLIED?

Your child will not tell you that he or she is being bullied in school because of the threats "Goliath" had voiced out. So, you will have to be observant of changes in your child's behavioural pattern. This is the key to knowing what your child is going through. A few of the signs to look out for in your child include the following:

1. **A lack of interest in school:** A child who is normally excited about going to school might suddenly begin to shy away by giving excuses of headaches, stomach trouble, etc. While there will be instances when your child *truly* has a headache, it is the *imaginary* ones you want to look out for.

Be sensitive when the headaches and stomach troubles become frequent - and the doctor cannot find anything particularly wrong! Do not ignore this or begin to nag the child (that is the last thing he or she needs at this time, believe me). Gently, but firmly, enquire from your child, or close school friends, what is going on in school.

2. **A change in behaviour:** Monitor the changes in your child's behaviour around this period in order to ascertain what is actually going on. Your child may be withdrawn, find it difficult to sleep properly or may start having nightmares. The child may loose his or her appetite, take it out on the younger ones at home or lose interest in the favourite things that were once loved and enjoyed.

3. **School performance:** If your child's performance in school work suddenly drops and the schoolwork begins to suffer; when the teacher calls you to register concern whereas it's never happened before, bullying may be the cause.

4. **Missing items at home:** If things start getting lost at home - items like money and toys - be alerted. Your child may be taking these things to the bullies to satisfy their demands and to protect himself or herself from their threats.

WHAT CAN YOU DO ABOUT IT?

If you have noticed any of the above signs in your child, do not take them lightly. There are some practical steps you can take to help the situation.

1. **Have a good relationship with your child.** It is important for parents to develop and establish a cordial relationship with their children. This will require an understanding of the difference between *fear* and *respect*.

God's Word commands children to respect their parents. However, God has not asked your children to be afraid of you. Your parental authority can be exercised effectively in a loving manner.

Gone are the days when parents rule their children by fear. If this is still your parenting style, your children will do things in your absence that you may never find out about. Why? Because they do not know how to relate to you. They do not know how you will react if they tell you what they are experiencing in life. They will, therefore, keep their hurts to themselves - and this is very dangerous if your child is being bullied.

Don't just be a parent, be a friend. Let your child trust you enough to make you a confidant and a counsellor. When I was growing up, I sometimes thought that my dad would beat me if I asked him for something. So, I would write what I wanted on a piece of paper and put it under his pillow, hoping for the best. That, of course, was not right. We all pray to God as our Father and are able to ask Him for the things we need.

A lot of children are suffering in silence and they want someone to talk to. The first thing you can do for *your* children to rescue them from bullies is to be that person they *can* talk to.   Improve on your parenting if you have to and lend your children a listening ear.

> *"Do not be harsh with your children lest they become discouraged" (Ephesians 6:4 GNB)*

Parenting success is the first hurdle you must overcome if you will help your child to cope with bullying. Once your children can relate freely with you, and you have established a solid relationship with them, most of the problems of bullying can easily be solved.

Educate your children about the importance of communicating with you no matter what the problem is. Have an open relationship with them; a relationship that will reassure them of security and protection. Your child must be able to say confidently, "My daddy will stand up for me!"

2. **Talk to the school authority.** When you have established that something is definitely wrong, book an appointment to talk to the school authority and firmly express your concern. Always document your feelings in writing. Let the school know that you will like a full investigation into the matter and want to be informed in writing. Also ask to see the school's policy concerning issues of this nature.

Your prayers will be more targetted by the information you receive about the matter. Once you have collected detailed information into what has happened, the people involved, what they have done and so on, you will be able to pray more effectively with God's Word.

3. **Keep Records.** File away the school's replies to your letters for future reference and watch out for any action they take.

4. **Keep a diary of events.** While you are tackling the issue with the authorities, encourage your child to tell you if any more bullying happens in school, and keep a day-to-day dairy of what is going on. Write down the details of what your child reports to you, the letters you write, the schools replies and the action taken.

5. **Pray.** Engage yourself in spiritual warfare, pulling down every stronghold; casting down every vain imagination that wants to exalt itself above God's knowledge in your child's life; arrest every situation that wants to oppress and torment your child. Pray against every adverse effect of bullying in your child.

6. **Assure your children.** Teach your children to read the word of God and pray everyday. Let them know that David was only a child when God delivered Goliath into his hands, and that they can rise above the onslaughts of bullies by the anointing and power of God.

If God helped David to defeat terrorists, He will surely help your child to conquer those who gang up against him in Jesus name.

"Shall the prey be taken from the mighty, or the lawful captive delivered? **But thus saith the Lord, even the captives of the mighty shall be taken away and the prey of the terrible shall be delivered. For I will contend with him that contendeth with thee and I will save thy children"** *(Isaiah 49:24-25 KJV).*

DO ALL YOU CAN

Do not leave any stone unturned. Pray for the bullies - that God will touch and change them; pray for their folks, for the school authority and all the actions and decisions that will be taken concerning the matter.

While you are still at it, pray for children worldwide who have had or are going through the same experience of being bullied, that the good Lord will heal their wounds and deliver them all.

As a Christian parent, do not underestimate the effects of bullying nor underrate the bullies. Do not say, "afterall, they are only children". Children they may be, but their aims are not in the favour of *your* children. Spring into action at the first trace of bullying. Give no place to the works of the devil.

Some children have been damaged psychologically and emotionally because of bullying. A few years ago, a secondary school Asian boy was found hanging in his bedroom because he could not handle his bullies. Instead of speaking out, he chose to end his life. May this not be our portion in Jesus' name.

SECTION TWO:

THE ISSUES

<u>SATAN-PROOF ISSUES 1-6</u>
INCLUDING THE FOLLOWING:

- FRIENDS OR FOES?
- BIRTHDAY PARTIES
- MUSIC
- TELEVISION
- SOAP OPERAS
- JEWELLERIES
- TATTOOS
- LANGUAGE
- IMAGE & OBJECT POWER
- FASHION & ACCESSORIES
- HAIRSTYLES & HAIRCUTS
- GIFTS FOOD
- OTHER PARTIES
- GAMES
- CARTOONS
- MOVIES
- SCHOOL JOURNEYS
- RACISM
- TOYS

CHAPTER FOUR

SATAN-PROOF ISSUES 1

FRIENDS OR FOES?

T HERE ARE many avenues through which Satan tries to attack and influence our children. Some are so subtle that the danger is not immediately evident. One of such avenues is friendships. If care is not taken, "child witchcraft" can operate amidst friendly relationships. (You may need to hear me out on this).

Satan, remember, is looking for anyone he can devour. Your children are easy targets - if you ignore his tactics of gaining control of their lives.

Some kids will choose to be friendly with your child in school. An attraction eventually develops which may be natural or intentional.

Notice that some "friends" will desire to be your child's best friend. They want to know your child's address and telephone number. Then they want to pay a visit to your child as often as possible. They love to share things with your child, entwining themselves to your child like parasites.

Mind you, I am not saying that all children friendships are foul but you will agree with me that some are. These are the kind that wriggle their way into your child's life until it is difficult to separate them when trouble arises. It will take discernment from the Holy Spirit for you to detect negative influences friends can have in your child's life. With His help you will discern those who come with specific objectives of gaining contol of your child's life. Their first step is to build trust, understand what your child likes or doesn't like and then the other steps follow.

GIFTS

Some friends will give your child all sorts of gifts at different times. Even though it is not your child's birthday neither is it Christmas time, they will still give them something.

The gifts may first be school writing utensils, like pens, pencils, rubbers or rulers. Then food items, like sweets, chocolates, biscuits and cakes. Then it graduates to jewellery items, like bangles, necklaces, earrings, hairbands, rings, badges, etc. Also, they can give your child books or pictures of themselves that they have drawn.

If you ask why your child has been given all these gifts, there will be a perfect explanation. Of course, all these could be innocent and straightforward, but you still need to be watchful.

An area of concern I have realised about this kind of friendship in school, is the sharing of drinks from the same bottle. We know that diseases and infections can be transfered through this means. You need to be careful as this happens all the time.

We need to screen our children's friends thoroughly and not only them, but their families and background. Pray for wisdom to be able to distinguish between what is suitable and what is not. If you can pick up a strange and funny vibe about any friendship, it probably is a *red alert signal* for you to intervene, cut the cord of friendship and declare your child's liberty.

A few years ago, one of my daughters would come home from school with a variety of gifts from a friend - perfume, handkerchief, teddy bears and so on. I got very uncomfortable and unsettled about this and had to do something about it. Whenever I saw these items I will throw them away.

My daughter did not see anything wrong with the gifts until I sat her down and had a long discussion with her. I educated her on the pros and cons of such gifts. Thank God she understood what I was talking about and learnt to say "no" to unusual gift offers.

Introducing or initiating a child into witchcraft can be done through gifts. But, glory be to God we are more than conquerors through Christ who loved us. We have overcome all kinds of evil by the blood of the lamb and by the word of our testimonies!

Every relationship that does not bear good fruit in our children must be rooted up and set ablaze with the fire of the Holy Spirit.

FOOD

Some children just love presenting themselves as "Santa Claus". They turn up everyday with sweets, bubble gums, and bars of chocolate to entice friends, classmates and schoolmates. You need to understand that some of these children come from occultic backgrounds and have been initiated into occultism from their nappy days. So, by school age they are perfect in the craft. They know what is irresistible to other children. What child will say "no" to sweeties?

A few years ago, a parent gave this testimony: Her five year old girl was given a polo mint trebor in school by another little girl her age. After a while, the girl who gave the trebor would appear to the parent's child in her sleep, wake her up and take her to a midnight conference.

However, because the parents of this innocent child are practising, prayerful Christians, God urged their child to tell them what was happening. She said to her mum, "Mum, you and dad should eat polo and come with me tonight. It is wonderful, I can fly!"

The mother screamed and enquired of her daughter who gave her the polo. Her daughter innocently mentioned the other girl's name. It turned out that the other girl was a child of a family friend -

someone they knew very well.

Hearing this, the bottom fell out of the mother. She alerted her husband and they both arranged a deliverance prayer for their daughter with their church pastor and the good Lord delivered her.

You need not wait to hear stories like this before you educate your children about the dangers of saying "yes" to everything.

BIRTHDAY PARTIES

In the context of eating food in school, a word about birthday parties is appropriate. Very often, a child or two will celebrate their birthdays in the classroom. They will bring party bags containing a packet of crisps, some assorted sweets, mini bars of chocolate, a balloon, a cup of drink, a toy, etc. Most of the time, they will also bring a cake.

As a member of the class, your child will participate in the birthday party. He will come home with a toy - having consumed the other items in that party bag!

Even though there is nothing wrong with celebrating birthdays, your child needs to learn to reserve things given to him for you to see and say a blessing over before consumption. Better still, teach and encourage your child to give God thanks for every meal, and to plead the blood of Jesus before eating. May God open your eyes of understanding.

OTHER PARTIES

I have started to observe a different twist to parties. A child who has brought things to school for his or her birthday party, might go a step further to invite each class member to come to his or her house for the "proper" birthday party. Lately, the parties are called names like a "sleep over" birthday party; a "slumber party"; "overnight" or "pyjama party"

During these parties, the children will mingle with each other; they will listen and dance to music, play games and chat a lot.

My children have brought home a couple of such ludicrous invitations and I have categorically said "No"! How can anyone underaged attend a sleepover party? For starters, you may not know much about the family of the birthday child or what their home looks like. You do not know where your child will sleep or what will happen while he or she is asleep.

Your first priority is your child's welfare and protection, so be very vigilant. A night of fun could turn into years of nightmare. These are things you can avoid, prevent and thank God for.

I would rather children were encouraged to go to all-night prayer meetings where they will receive a fresh anointing of God and be blessed than go to a "Night club in embryo".

MUSIC

Have you listened to the kind of music your child is interested in lately? Do you think it is suitable for moral and spiritual development? Will this kind of music fulfil God's purpose for your child's life?

When I was growing up, the music we used to listen to and enjoy was considerably clean. You could hear clearly what the artiste was singing about and could dance to the music sensibly, dress modestly and respectably too.

Today, when I hear the music sold to the society, I feel a lot of it is an insult to people's intelligence. It is difficult to sort out the rhythm of the music, the language is foul and negative, and most importantly, they do not glorify God.

A child of God should know what to listen to. When a musician sings a song like "Killing me softly with this song" and your child stands in agreement with the musician by singing and dancing along, fulfilling the scripture that said, "Where two or three shall agree", the result cannot be pallatable.

Screen the type of music that your child listens to and how they dance to it. Also be wise about invitations to "sleepover parties" (discussed above) because you do not know the kind of music that will be played and danced to. there

GAMES

Children enjoy playing games with each other, they do this in schools, at parties, at home and even in Sunday schools.

Games are simple, straightforward ways children have fun. There are many good things children gain from playing games. The most important is the reinforcement of concepts and skills acquired in their learning process. It also helps them take turns and to apply reasoning. It is a way to do problem-solving and investigative work.

There are a variety of games in the shops these days that might teach children one concept or the other but the names given to some of them bothers me. A family friend gave my children a Christmas present a couple of years ago. We felt it was a game in the Christmas wrapper but kept it till Christmas day to open it. On Christmas morning, we gathered around, had our quiet time, prayed over all the Christmas presents and began to rip the wrappers open one by one with excitement.

My oldest daughter opened the gift from our family friend and suddenly exclaimed, "Mum!". I looked up and was equally shocked. The present was a game all right, but the name on it said *Frustration!*. I thank God for my children's reaction. My six year old shouted, "No way! We have to throw this game into the bin!"

So with all the empty boxes and wrappers of the

other presents, we threw this game of "Frustration" out of our home!

Another game I saw in the shop is called *Jeopardy*. I wonder why the manufacturers name their products this way. I pray that our children will never play or have an encounter with *frustration* and *jeopardy* in Jesus name, amen.

CHAPTER FIVE

SATAN-PROOF ISSUES 2

TELEVISION

THE MEDIA plays an active part in the development of our children in diverse ways. Every programme has a message to pass across to them. The kind of messages communicated can either build or destroy. Sadly, most themes aired are worldly.

Some people are of the opinion that television is not good for spiritual growth and that Christians should not own one. Such people will not allow their children to watch television or go to cinemas.

While I respect individual opinions, the fact is that you cannot monitor your child every hour of the day. If children do not watch television at home, they will watch it at school, a friend's house or somewhere beyond your watchful eyes.

Besides, if you do not allow your kids on the street, then there must be something to give them that will amuse them at home.

Another fact is that as an intercessor (and every believer should be one), you need to be current with world affairs in order to know how to target your prayers. The television can serve as the information bureau of an intercessor. Television, therefore, has its own advantage and cannot be written off outright.

There are a lot of programmes on television these days and most of them are unsuitable for the eyes and minds of a Christ-centred child. Parents need to educate their children seriously and pray that their eyes will not behold evil.

The television is a teacher. Its "curriculum" or "programme of study" has consequences for your children. Part of the television's "curriculum" is violence, bad language and strong immoral subjects. It is vital that you do not allow your children to watch just about anything on the TV. Some parents feel it is a way of getting children occupied so they don't get bothered. But if you do not educate your children on what to watch and what not to watch, you may be doing them a lot of damage.

The devil uses a lot of programmes on the television these days to "evangelise" for his evil kingdom. He features in music, advertisements, documentaries, talk shows, movies, and fashion shows. Even the children channels are becoming contaminated with evil representations.

CARTOONS

It used to be safe and fun for children to watch cartoons. Even adults found cartoons amusing. But nowadays, it is a subtle way Satan uses to pollute the minds of Children. The producers even have the nerve to introduce "Cult cartoons"! The creatures used in some cartoons look so strange, the way they talk is scary and their colours, eek! Cartoon characters are now spooky and eerie and have demonic motives behind them. Even their storylines are abnormal and satanic.

I disallow my children from watching most cartoons on TV. (I say "most" because they are allowed to watch "Tom and Jerry" and a few others that are considerably safe compared to the ones in question). The fact of the matter is you don't let your children get obsessed with cartoons.

SOAP OPERAS

What about soap operas? There are a lot of soap operas on television propagating that it is right for young children and teenagers to compromise and go into unsuitable, immoral relationships; that teenage pregnancies are OK; that it is alright for a child to disobey and scream at their parents; that it is alright for young children to engage in gang activities.

In one soap opera show, a priest commits fornication and visits a public house to have a drink. A Christ-centred child must not find soap operas like these funny or amusing.

Its what you teach your children that they will follow. If you are a "soap" addict, they will grow to become addicts themselves. Check the level of morality in the things you expose them to and educate them on a continual basis about what the Bible teaches and commands.

MOVIES

These days, movies have been divided into different categories. The categories are:

U - Universal

PG - Parental Guidance

12 - 12 years and above.

15 - 15 years and above.

18 - 18 years and above

X - X-rated (Adult movies)

The U movies mean that everyone can watch safely. PG movies imply that viewing depends on parental tastes and beliefs. You may not want your own child to watch it, while another parent may think otherwise. The television producers feel it is suitable for everyone but also respect the differing opinions of parents.

X-rated films are clearly immoral. They are packed full of temptation, nudity and sex, and are absolutely not suitable for Christians - adults and children. Every responsible parent will make sure that the children are protected from devilish influences that come through these kind of films.

Tim is an eight year old child. His mother is a Christian but his father an unbeliever. Tim was exposed to X-rated films from an early age by his dad. Contrary to the mum's desire, Tim's dad allowed him to watch anything he wanted on TV.

The dad claimed that Tim had great potential and needed to know all about intimacy from adult movies. The dad did not stop there, but also took Tim to the casino and taught him how to gamble. As a result of this lifestyle, Tim stayed up late most of the time.

The evidence of all this was that Tim always came to class with puffy, tired-looking eyes. He would doze, yawn and stretch during lessons.

Tim's teacher once asked the class to draw and label a basic part of the human body during science. Tim drew a man's penis with semen gushing out! The picture was shown to the headteacher who called in the boy's mother for questioning. The mum came, with tears in her eyes, to defend herself. Nothing else was done about the matter.

Tim never concentrated in class; he daydreamt a lot and dropped considerably in his school performance. What was so shocking was that when confessing to what he did with his dad, Tim threw his hands in the air, shrugged his shoulders and said,

"Its no big deal! It's only television". "Violence on TV is funny", he said. With tear-filled eyes, Tim's teacher stood speechless, wondering why a little boy should be exposed to immorality from an early age.

SAFE TV

For young children, there are a lot of lovely programmes on T.V. that feature boys and girls taking part in a simple learning activity.

An example of these children's programmes is *Blue Clues,* which helps children to solve puzzles and learn at the same time. Another one is *Nick Junior* which features children learning to do some shopping, cooking, or colouring. Another good programme is *Barneys,* for older children.

There are some considerably sensible programmes for teenage and older children. I think it depends on what parents feel about them. Examples are *Sister, Sister, Moesha, Smart Guy* and *Keenan and Kel.* These programmes, at least, promote family values and morality. The parents featured in these comedies are shown to be responsible and concerned about their children's behaviour. Again watching these television programmes depends on the views of individual parents.

We have cable TV at home and have access to about 20 channels. I, therefore, have ministered strongly to my children the spiritual implications of watching the wrong programme. I told them that they will be showing and proving to me how much self-control and maturity they have by not watching something unsuitable in my absence.

If you agree with your children on what they can and cannot watch, they will avoid violence, bad language and immorality. Their minds will be protected from the garbage that is polluting our world through the TV screen.

CHAPTER SIX

SATAN-PROOF ISSUES 3

FASHION AND ASSESORIES

ONE WAY to distinguish mad people in Africa is the clothes they wear - torn rags. Interestingly, this is what seems to be in vogue today. Check out modern-day fashion - people are crazy about torn T-shirts and Jeans. Everywhere you look these days, someone is wearing something that you cannot comprehend. You then begin to wonder, in a shop full of lovely clothes, why choose a "rag"?

A lot of television presenters, celebrities and showbiz people do not help matters as they are the ones young people see as role models. These television showbiz gurus go to the shops and buy clothes too small for their sizes, squeeze into them, expose two thirds of the bodies, and call their outfits "designer clothes".

It is not right for God's children to dress provo-catively because, *"Our body is the temple of God, the Holy Spirit dwells in us"*. In all that we do, it should be our priority to glorify the Father. Parents should monitor what their children wear or want to wear, especially if they are the ones to foot the biil!

Children will want to copy the latest fashion in order to look and dress like celebrities or friends. It is the duty of parents and guardians to point them in the right direction.

Some children will understand and take it in good faith when a parent explains why they cannot have certain things. Others will sulk and throw tantrums. Whatever the reaction of the child, let it be known, gently and yet firmly, that you will not compromise or bargain with their emotions to purchase for them something contrary to the will of God for them. Soon they will learn not to put a demand on you for something they cannot get.

If a child learns at an early age that they are children of the Most High; that they need to develop reverence for God, develop self respect, self control and a sound mind, that child will grow with confidence and self esteem. He or she will not depart from this respectable way in adulthood. People who wear "see throughs" and clothes that expose two-thirds of the body may tell you it makes them feel good, whereas the real motive is for "attention". They are "attention seekers", the "notice-me-I-am-around" type.

You do not need to wear "see throughs" to feel good about yourself. Jesus who lives in you, the hope of glory, will make you feel great. A child needs to know this. I am not saying you should dress your children in "Mary Slessor" clothes! Dress them modestly. Teach them to respect themselves first, and others will in turn give them respect.

JEWELLERIES

For centuries past, women have worn earrings, necklaces, bracelets and bangles. Even Bible women did. It is common for women to wear jewelleries, particularly, earrings. Men also wear jewelleries - necklaces, bracelets etc - but normally they do not wear earrings.

These days, if you go to jewellery shops, there are a lot of men's earrings on display and I wonder what is the significance?

As if this is not puzzling enough, you can now find earnings worn everywhere - on the tongue, the navel, breasts, eyebrows, nose and so on. Where next? As Christians, we should all wonder when all these "Amalekites" came to town advertising their fashion which by the way, can be occultic and very demonic.

A television comedian once came on air and said to his audience that his son had his navel pierced (ouch!). The moment this was complete, the man who did the piercing was quoted saying, "Good! One more of us, one less of them!" Heavy words, isn't it?

Can you grasp the spiritual implication of what the man said, "One more of us, One less of them"? I felt sorry for the man relating this experience because he did not understand what he was talking about. He said it jokingly with a loud, throaty laugh. How sad.

What is the implication of this for Christian children? Some children in your child's school belong to "Amalekite" family units and will flaunt what they have in the face of others. Your son might think it is "cool" as well. But God will give you the wisdom to explain the odds in this to them. Even a lot of teachers are allowed to teach children these days with piercings all over their bodies.

I used to know a male teacher who was in charge of 3-year old nursery kids. This teacher had earrings on his eyes, nose and ears. He even boasted to another teacher that he had one on his nipple and another one on his navel. What kind of a role model would this teacher be to the children he teaches? Knowing what children are like, some will dare to touch the rings, and I can bet he allowed them to do so. Only God can rescue and protect our children from teachers like this.

This same teacher confessed to being an ex-punk gang member. He even brought a picture of what he used to look like - hair shaved with a bit in the middle, and coloured bright orange. Boy! Was it scary! Even though he is now a teacher, the traits of his former self lingers on. Are you getting the picture? You need to pray that your child will not have an encounter with evil in Jesus name.

Dear parents, let us *Satan-proof our children!* We should not be too wrapped up with our own needs and circumstances, worrying about things of this world, and neglecting the God-given responsibility we have to take care of them. We must not give Satan a chance to steal, kill and destroy that which is a treasure in our lives and precious to God.

Satan's strategy of plundering the lives of children is to make parents so busy that they have no time to watch over them. This will not be our portion in Jesus' name, Amen. We are God's stewards and will one day account for everything He has entrusted into our care, including our children.

HAIRSTYLES & HAIRCUTS

God created the hair on our head and knows how many strands are there. None of them will fall off without His knowledge. When a woman fixes her hair, she looks and feels good. When a man has a haircut, he looks refreshed. Children, of course, with excitement, love to show off their new haircuts.

Everyone has a preferred choice of hairdo. Some women choose to wear perms, curls, short cuts, plaits, weave-ons, wigs, etc. Some men belong to the "Samson club" - the no-razor-shall-touch-my-head group; some prefer short hair, while others prefer a total shave off.

While children like to change the way they look, the general rule to apply should be to glorify God in everything, even in the style of hair we wear for them. These days, however, the styles you find on school children is shocking.

Children love to wear hairstyles with lots of patterns and inscriptions, many of them strange looking. After a haircut, a remnant of hair is carved out like a calabash, and words like "Wicked", "Nike", etc. are spelt out on the back of the head. Sometimes its the picture of a snake or an alien that is carved out. No doubt, when the demons attached to these symbols see them, they rejoice - "Fresh meat!" - and they trail along.

What about girls hair? If you go into beauty salons, you will find a variety of hair extensions. People are no longer satisfied with the colour of hair God created them with. They want assorted colours, styles and looks. Walking on the street, you will see young girls of secondary school age with patches of red, green, yellow or orange. Some will even go as far as dying the whole hair bright red.

What is the significance of this latest fashion? Have we not borrowed and adopted the fashion of the skinhead punks? Incidentally, these absurd-looking "painted hairstyles" is what you will find on some cartoon characters.

Hair extensions, on the other hand, come as human hair or synthetic hair. The human hair extensions are indeed real human hair. Have we asked ourselves who the hair belonged to? Are the owners alive or dead?

A lot of people prefer to use real human hair extensions for themselves and their children. Do not get me wrong here; I am not saying you have committed a crime by using them. Its just that we are children of the kingdom of heaven and God expects us to apply godly wisdom in all our endeavours, especially where it concerns children.

Some years ago, a man of God, preaching at a church crusade, emphatically warned Christian women to be careful of human hair extensions. Firstly, you do not know who donated it to the business world, what kind of people they were, and the things they practised in life. Secondly, according to the claim of the man of God, not all of these human hair extensions are ordinary. This was the experience the minister once had:

While ministering to a woman in a deliverance service, he laid his hand on the woman's head and started to pray. Amazingly, a few strands of the human hair she was wearing clustered on his fingers and stung him like a snake. He had to be prayed for by other ministers before the effect of the attack was neutralised.

You may find the experience of this man of God a bit out of the ordinary. However, in matters relating to your children, you can never be too careful. Children are innocent and naturally beautiful. They do not need strange human hair extensions to enhance their beauty. *"Every good and perfect gift comes from heaven"*, and children are a gift from God, "fearfully and wonderfully made".

At home, I use synthetic hair extensions for myself and for my children. Even then, we still plead the blood of Jesus on them before use.

TATTOOS

A tattoo is a coloured design on the skin made by pricking it with needles. An area of the skin is cut into a desired pattern. This cutting involves the shedding of blood from the area cut. Tattoos originated from blood covenants and rituals performed during idol worship. Eventually, they developed into fashion.

I call tattoos *subtle evil evangelisation* because if you look closely at the designs people wear, you will see the images of animals, eastern gods and inscriptions of evil. Usually, you will find tattoos on adults' arms, legs or other parts of the body. Some tattoos can be peeled or washed off. Others are permanent.

The sad thing is that some children are made to go through this agony so they can have a symbol or image on them. Innocently, some of these children are marked for evil in the name of fashion. If the tattoo is parmanent, they will carry this mark for the rest of their lives. As if this is not horrifying enough, there is a kind of bubble gum in the market now where tattoo kits are included!

A child came to my house and on his left arm, was a tattoo of a skull. When I spotted it, I asked him where he got it from. "Inside the wrapper of a bubble gum", he said.

I pointed out to this child what a skull stood for - death and danger. I then asked him to scrub it off immediately and never to come into my house with such symbols again.

If a Christian child develops an interest in tattoos, he or she will pester the parents for that bubble gum in order to have a tattoo.

The tattoo of the world is visible and clearly evil, but the "tattoo" of God's children is invisible and purifying. Perhaps you are wondering what I mean. The Bible says in proverbs 7:3, "Keep my teaching with you all the time, write it on your head". Another place reads, *"They will each mark the name of the Lord on their arms"* (Isaiah 44:5c).

The children of the world may have their own mark, but we have the mark of the blood of Jesus. "Henceforth, let no man trouble us for we bear in our body the mark of Jesus"!

We must not stand by and watch our children, young or old, follow evil fashion. If their counterparts in school are identified with the mark of evil, Christian children must be identified with the mark and fingerprints of God. If your child likes and wants a tattoo, gently but firmly minister to him or her why it cannot be done.

CHAPTER SEVEN

SATAN-PROOF ISSUES 4

LANGUAGE

LANGUAGE IS the most important means of communication. Whether it is spoken or written, we get messages across to other people using a particular language. The way we use language is important because what we say can be understood or misunderstood; interpreted or misinterpreted. Sometimes we are straightforward and sometimes complicated.

We all speak different languages depending on our location in the world. In spite of the differences, we have found a way of communicating with one another. The goal in communication is to pass a message across to the hearer without confusion.

The language school children are adopting today is very worrying and baffling. A lot of slangs and terminologies are used that do not make sense. When children are given a task on "Words and Opposites" to do in class, they usually find it difficult. However, when they speak amongst themselves, they say quite the opposite of what they mean.

As parents, we should not be ignorant of the devil's devises. This is another area where he is working subtly. Satan knows what the word of God says about the words we speak.

> *"You will have to live with the consequences of everything you say. What you say can preserve life or destroy it. So you must accept the consequences of your words"* (Proverbs 18:20 GNB).

The devil is turning most children against themselves by making them say and accept that which is not in line with God's Word.

For instance, when a teacher sets a task for children in the classrooms, some children will say, "I *can't* do this", or "it's too *hard*" - even after the task has been discussed step by step and questions have been raised. When children say they *can't*, I always remind them that they "can do *all things* through Christ Jesus who strengthens" them.

If a child does not fully understand a task, a teacher will explain it all over again. If it is still too complicated, we employ what we call *Differentiation*, which means, simplifying a task for a child to manage. Differentiation might be carried out when a child truly does not grasp a concept.

In my experience as a teacher, however, there are groups of children who just do not want to do anything, no matter how straightforward a task is. These children like to influence others in the class. They disrupt the class and distract other children. I constantly minister to children in this category because they do not like to think. They hate reasoning. Their easy way out is, "*I can't*". There is a difference between "*I can't*" and "*I won't*". If they say, "*I won't*", then a teacher knows that they are not interested in working.

A child in my class once told me, "you know something Miss, I hate thinking. I just want to do something that won't make me think". I was shocked to hear this because the essence of being a human being is the ability to think and reason. This child will always copy other children's work because that was the easy way out for her. A parent should point out to the children that every human being has been given the ability to find ways of solving problems. Your child does not have to run away from challenges.

I once asked my class a question: "What will you do if a lion suddenly appears in the playground? Will you just stand there or will you quickly think of a way of escape?". I got a lot of answers from the children. From their answers I made them realise that when they are presented with a task, they ought to immediately apply their sense of reasoning to find ways of tackling the problem. All a teacher wants to see is children having a go at their work. "Never say, *I can't!*", I told them.

Other confusing uses of language includes the use of the word *afraid*.

"I'm afraid he is not here right now".

"I'm afraid I can't come to your house".

"I'm afraid it got broken".

"I'm afraid you can't come to my party".

I'm afraid! I'm afraid! I'm afraid!

Afraid of what? God says He has not given us the Spirit of fear. Why should you be afraid?

Another phrase commonly used is, "That's *wicked* man!". You will hear this from the lips of most children. They now think this is the ultimate way of passing compliments. I cannot recount how many times in my class or across the school that children have passed compliments to me using this phrase. Each time I try to correct them, but they carry on using the phrase.

Children would say, "Miss I like your shoes, they are wicked", or "I like your hairdo, it's *wicked*".

My response has always been, "Is it? If it's *wicked* looking, I better take them off!".

"No! You do not understand. We mean its good", they will say.

"Why didn't you say that in the first place. I'll hate to wear anything *wicked!*". At this, they will always laugh, probably mocking that I am not abreast with the latest terminology.

As a teacher, I take it very serious. I have also realised that correcting and educating them once is not enough. I, therefore, continue to remind them of this error and how they can correct it. Anything wicked is not of God but from the devil, and we must not allow our children to speak evil.

Satan has used the influence of music stars to pervert the language of children. One artiste sang a song titled "Bad" and most people, especially children, fell for it. "Bad is now a slang used by children as they all echo the lyrics to the song, "You know I'm bad; I'm bad you know it; Whose bad?"

The devil is definitely the one who is bad. Do not allow your children to negatively confess that they are bad. Educate them with the truths in the word of God. Let your children know that words are important - that it reflects what is inside them.

> *"A good person brings good out of the treasure of good things in his heart; a bad person brings bad out of his treasure of bad things.* **For the mouth speaks what the heart is full of"** *(Luke 6:45).*

Some children cannot say a sentence without using swear words. More and more school children are thinking it is "cool" to speak vile. They carelessly use four letter words that do not edify. Generally, children have not learnt how to converse with each other. They tend to shout themselves down during discussions. It is in the middle of arguments and word-exchanges that most of these foul talk come out.

Children now address one another as "idiots", "bastards", "Stupid", etc. They are fond of calling each other horrible names. More than once I have heard little children come out with things like "Your mother is a transsexual"; "Your mother is a lesbian"; "You are a big fat cow". Aren't children supposed to be innocent? From where do they get all these vocabulary?

As I mentioned in the introduction of this book, children are influenced by the environment in which they grow, and by the people they relate to. Children who indulge in filthy language have copied it from somewhere. It is your duty as parent to teach your children how to communicate graciously.

Minister to your children and let them know that their body is the temple of God, and that the Holy Spirit dwells in them. They do not want to grieve the Holy Spirit, their best friend, by speaking the language of this world.

Correct them persistently. I take a lot of time correcting children in my class. Do not give up on your own children too. As I have said many times in this book, intensify your prayers for your kids.

Proverbs 10:19,21 GNB

"The more you talk, the more likely you are to sin. If you are wise you will keep quiet"

"A good person's words will benefit many people, but you can kill yourself with stupidity"

Psalm 141:3-4 GNB

"Lord, place a guard at my mouth a sentry at the door of my lips. Keep me from wanting to do wrong and from joining evil people in their wickedness. May I never take part in their feasts."

TOYS

Toys are miniature images of real life objects - human beings, birds, insects, inanimate objects, etc. Children love playing around with them. Some toys have given kids pleasure for hundreds of years.

Toy animals have always been favourites among children. In ancient Greece, children played with wooden animals whose tails wagged or whose jaws clashed together when pulled with a string. They also had jointed dolls made of clay, with arms that could be moved by chords.

The Egyptians had flat wooden dolls with beads for hair and no legs. Some of the early Roman dolls were made of rags. The most popular toy, "the teddy bear" did not come into existence until the beginning of the 20th century. They got their name from a baby bear caught by Theodore Roosevelt, then the president of the United States, when he was hunting in the Rocky Mountains. The incident was portrayed at the time in a newspaper cartoon with the caption "teddy's Bear".

These days toys are made out of a variety of materials ranging from wool, metal, plastic, wood, etc. Irrespective of the material used to make toys, the bottom line is that they are fashioned in the image of something or someone - and this is an issue that needs investigation.

IMAGE POWER

God made us in His own image and breathed the breath of life into us, after which we began to function as living beings. Having being created by God, and imparted into by Him, we were purposed to function according to His will.

The image of a thing represents the object it resembles. If it contains life through impartation (as was the case of Adam), then it has the *power* to fulfil the purposes and desires of the one who created it.

What is the importance of this? Parents need to take note of the kind of toys they buy for their children and the kind of toys the children are given for birthdays, Christmas and other festive periods. Check what kind of toy a friend gives to your child in school or the kind of toy thrown into their happy meal in Mac Donald's! What image is the toy portraying? Who or what is empowering it to gain influence over your child?

OBJECT POWER

Even inanimate objects can be empowered. There are various instances in the Bible where God has empowered inanimate objects with His anointing to perform. The rod of Moses, for instance, was used to perform miracle after miracle in Egypt and in the wilderness; Samson used an ordinary jawbone of a donkey to kill one thousand men; God used a bronze snake to heal the Israelites when they were bitten by poisonous snakes.

With these few Biblical examples, you can see that inanimate objects can be used for specific purposes. In the case of the metal snake, a mere look had a lasting effect.

If God uses inanimate objects to fulfil one function or another, what stops Satan from counterfeiting this act? Where there is an original, there will also be a copy. It is a known fact that objects are dedicated to the devil for occultic and satanic purposes.

I recently watched a video series that exposed the activity of witches. They would change from their natural image into animals like owls, dogs, wolves etc. What I want you to understand is that when these undercover spirits see an image they can identify with, they consider it an open invitation to enter. A lot of toys are made in the image of these braggarts. An example is the image of a mermaid.

A family friend lives with her six year old son whose favourite toys are horrid-looking toys. He has a row of these "evil" figures on the showcase of their living room. Even though this woman is a prayerful Christian, she allowed the collection of the toys in order to please her son.

One day, when visiting her, I saw an array of fierce-looking warlords in the house. I asked her why they had them and she replied by saying that her son loved collecting them. Gently and respectfully, I pointed out to her the kind of things she was allowing into her home, the atmosphere they create, and the effect they may have on the child.

At this, she confessed that her son was not sleeping well, was rebellious at home and wanted his way all the time. It was in a bid to keep peace that she bought some of those images for him. The rest he had collected from the gift pack of a fast food restaurant.

I suggested that she confiscated all of the toys and replaced them with educational toys. She felt very reluctant because she did not want to upset her son. Some of the toys were not even at home because the son had taken them to school.

Eventually, after ministering to this woman about the importance of disinfecting her home with the blood of Jesus and getting rid of the property of Beelzebub, we took every single toy and threw them in the big dustbin beside her apartment. When we met a few weeks later, she testified to the goodness of God, that her son was now sleeping through the night and had started to calm down. Praise the Lord!

Be careful of the dolls, action heroes and monster toys that you allow your child to play with. They can affect young minds and influence their character.

Electronic toys also need to be screened thoroughly as manufacturers have infested the market with a variety of unedifying video games and visual entertainment. While I have not given much attention to video games, the names of some are indications of evil. I saw a few disturbing ones displayed on shop windows. One is called *Voodoo* and another *Destroyer*. Why would you allow your children to *play* with *Voodoo*?

There are times when your child will be given a toy to play with in school by a friend. Even though it is against the school policy, children bring toys into school everyday. Most of the toys they bring are small and easy to hide in their coats, pockets, or pencil cases.

Educate your children about these things. *Prevention is better than cure.* Do not let your child perish for a lack of knowledge.

Have you decorated your children's room with assorted toys and are their beds stuffed with a variety of objects? Take a closer look at each of them, and pray for wisdom and discernment. If the Holy Spirit convicts you about any of them, do not mind the cost - throw them away!

CHAPTER EIGHT

SATAN-PROOF ISSUES 5

RACISM

*T*HE EARTH *is the Lords and the fullness thereof; the world and they that dwell therein. For he hath founded it upon the seas and established it upon the floods."* This classic Scripture tells us that God is the Ultimate Landlord, not only of the earth, but of the universe in its entirety. He created diverse kinds of people and gave them an equal "tenancy agreement" to occupy the earth.

There are groups of people, however, who feel that others are second-class creatures that should not exist in the world. Such people place themselves on a pedestal of superiority over humanity. They have programmed their minds for many generations to discriminate against people different from themselves. Such people we call racists.

In the Bible, stories of racism abound. The Moabites, Edomites and Amorites, refused to let the Israelites pass through their land. They discriminated against God's people and would not let them into their territories (Numbers 21 and 22).

In Genesis 26, Isaac, the son of Abraham, was deported by Abimelech King of Philistines to Gerar (vs 16), because Isaac was prospering too much on his land. They proved to Isaac by this action that they had right to the land.

In Exodus 1:8-22, the children of Israel were severely discriminated against in Egypt. Read some of the details of their ordeal.

> *"Now there arose up a new King over Egypt which knew not Joseph. And he said unto his people, Behold, the people of the children of Israel are mightier than we. Come on let us deal wisely with them; lest they multiply and it come to pass that when there falleth out any war, they join also unto our enemies and fight against us and so get them up out of the land.* **Therefore they did set over them taskmasters to afflict them with their burdens.** *And they built for Pharaoh treasure cities, Rithom and Raamses.* **And the Egyptians made the children of Israel to serve with rigour.** *And they made their lives bitter with hard bondages in mortar and in brick and n all manner of service in the field, all their service where in they made them serve, was with rigour..."*

Egyptian midwives were assigned to monitor pregnant Israelite women and to snuff the life out of every baby boy they deliver. The purpose was to keep the Israelites from growing in number, strength and power.

From this story, you can see how racism affects even children. The devil will always try to maintain a minority mentality, not only among the older generation, but also among children.

Moreover, the Egyptians made the Jews serve with rigour. The kind of jobs open to them were the odd ones, with hard labour. The Israelites were not given high positions in the society. They were not considered good enough to be directors or managers.

The picture is essentially the same of today's world. Some sections of the society have been tagged "ethnic minority groups".

You may ask what all this has to do with your children. The truth is that most of the children from "ethnic minority" families face racism everyday in school - from their peer group, school helpers and sometimes from class teachers.

MANIFESTATIONS OF RACISM

Racism is practised in schools in a variety of ways, directly or indirectly. A racist can sometimes be open and blunt about his or her feelings against someone of a different background or skin colour. At other times, feelings may not be verbalised, but that which is in the heart manifests in their actions.

Others decide to go the "pity-them" way. They get friendly with you in a sympathetic manner, feel sorry for you and make you feel they can just about tolerate you. Racists can be old or young, male or female, and they are found in all walks of life.

A child may be called names because of his or her skin colour or background. Names like "Monkey", "Paki", "Vanilla Ice Cream", "Nigger", "Chinko", or "Chimpanzie" are common.

Others, especially bilingual children (those who have English as a second language), may have their accent laughed at or mimicked. They get told they are stupid and funny because of the way they speak. As a result, they shy away from sharing their ideas in class discussions. They would prefer to be quiet and avoid other children laughing at them.

Imagine the trauma some children experience just because English is not their mother tongue. Children who suffer from racist attacks will tend to shy away from the school environment. As a parent, you should look out for the symptoms discussed under bullying (see page 39). Sometimes, racism and bullying cannot be separated as one of the motives for bullying a child could be because he is different from others.

RACISM AMONG CHILDREN

A few years ago I taught a class of six and seven year olds. During science lesson, we treated a topic titled "The Environment". I asked the children to write what they felt about their immediate environment (the school environment), the things they enjoyed and those they would like to change.

After the task, I selected a few children to share what they had written. Some of them wanted a big park with funfair; some would love to see play things on the playground like see-saws, merry-go-rounds, and so on. A boy then came forward and shocked the whole class. This is a paraphrase of what he wrote:

"There are too many black children buzzing around the school. They make me sick to the pit of my stomach. The change I would like to see is for all black children to suddenly disappear so that the school environment will be reserved only for white people."

You can imagine this coming from a seven year-old boy. After the intial shock, there was an uproar among the children, especially from the "black children" the boy was attacking with his pen. They wanted to break every bone in his body! By God's grace we were able to arrest the situation.

I calmed everybody down and we carried on with classwork. During dinner, I called the boy and had a serious chat with him. "What gave you the idea that some people should not be in school?", I asked him. "It's my dad", he replied. "He doesn't like none of your people".

"Why does daddy hate black people?", I asked.

"I don't know", was his reply.

I then asked him a direct question: "If you get knocked down by a car, God forbid, and it was a black doctor who could assist you to regain your health, would you rather die?". "No", he said, "I would not like to die".

Afterwards, I filled in the Incident Form and took the boy to the headteacher. His parents were invited for a meeting and he was suspended for three days. When he came back, his views did not change.

There are more children in school that have the same opinion as this boy. These are the same children who study and play with your children in school. Imagine your children playing with people who wish that something bad should happens to them! These secret "wishes" result into incidents like tripping a child over on purpose and claiming it was an accident.

It is important that you cover your child with the blood of Jesus always, and cancel every vain imagination that is contrary to God's plan for their lives. Pray that God will protect them from the calculated attacks of those that hate them.

CAN A CHILD RACIST BE HELPED?

Recently, a boy had a misunderstanding with a chinese boy in my class over something very trivial. This boy then said to the chinese boy, "I don't like none of you people, you don't belong here". As it was near playtime, I sent the children out to play. When they came back, I suddenly wrote on a flip chart: *"The earth is the Lord's and the fullness thereof"*.

The children (nine and ten year olds) went all quiet, paid attention and wondered why I had written this.

When I asked the class what they understood by the statement, there was a long silence. After a while, a girl (obviously from a Christain background) said, "I think it means God is the owner of the earth". Although she was right, *"the fullness thereof"* part of the statement was a bit tricky for her. I then explained to the children that God is the Ultimate Landlord of the universe and that He created everything in the world.

"When you were born," I asked them, "did you come into the world with a piece of land marked 'MINE' in your hands?" They all laughed, not yet figuring why we were having the discussion.

I explained that the same land spreads all over the world; the same air blows on people; water tastes the same everywhere; and people everywhere have the same features.

"How many of you like salad?", I asked. Most hands went up. "Do you know that a bowl of salad contains a mixture of vegetables that are coloured differently? It is the unity of the vegetables that brings out the beautiful flavour of the salad". At this illustration, all the children started to clap.

I gave more illustrations - tea, milk and sugar have different colours but come together to produce a nice, warm drink; the zoo has many species of animals in the same environment and they are allowed to make their respectful noises without one being shouted down by another.

After all the illustrations, I gently refferred to the incidence that occured before playtime and asked if the boy was justified. The whole class said "No!". Eventually, the boy genuinely apologised to the Chinese boy and the class lived happily ever after!

The point here is that most children who pass racist comments can be educated because they do it in ignorance. I have told my children not to react angrily to such things because racists need our sympathy; they are locked in the "prison of the mind"; they suffer from "knowledge deficiency".

Once you take time to explain to them, some will learn and others will turn a deaf ear. Educate your children on how to guard their precious hearts from being wounded by racist comments, and how to react in love. Intercede for them so that they will not grow up as racists themselves. Children are innocent and trusting. It is the adults around them that pollute and poison their minds against others.

TEACHER RACISTS

Unfortunately, there are many racists teaching children in schools. There is probably one, at least, in every school! These adults are biased and prejudiced against children of a different race from theirs. They have been so from childhood.

Children who find themselves in the tentacles of a

teacher racist are always in trouble; they are always the ones picked on, no matter how they try to please their teacher. Racist teachers will constantly abuse, accuse, curse, reprimand and intimidate a child that falls into the category of "different". These teachers will never write anything encouraging in the school report of their victims.

When these children become under-achievers, they are recommended as "special needs" children. In the negative sense, this means that a child is a slow learner, has learning disabilities or behavioural problems. A lot of the times, parents hardly bother to investigate why their children are not doing well at school. Instead, they will sign the dotted lines in agreement with the school that their child needs "special education". With their own hands, they put their child in the prison of hopelessness (read more about "special needs" in chapter 11).

Racism is not easy to conceal. A teacher once said that a biological virus will soon be released into the atmosphere, designed to wipe out all ethnic minority groups, like Africans and Indians. Would such a person find teaching "ethnic minority" children a delightful task?

One teacher made life difficult for a particular child in his class. He terrified this child and reduced him to a nervous wreck. He would always pick on the child and even went to the extent of recording the child's screams and cries on tape! The parents of this child had no clue of what their son was going through in school everyday.

Another child always got in trouble with his teacher. He probably spent more time in the company of the headteacher than in his class learning. He became famous in school for being "stupid".

I found this boy in front of the headteacher's office one afternoon and asked him to come and see me. The next morning, he came into my class and I had a chat with him about his behaviour.

"Miss, I do not cause trouble in class", he said. "My teacher, Miss Venice, just likes pinning every blame on me and I do not know why". At this the boy bursted into tears. In between sobs, he said, "My parents are threatening to take me back to my home country because of a letter Miss Venice wrote to them about my behaviour".

I felt compassion for the boy. The fact that he could cry showed that he had a soft heart and could be spoken to. I took time to minister to him and suggested ways he could turn the table around against his "assailant". The simple suggestions I gave him included the following:

1. Obey every class rule and regulation.

2. Listen whenever Miss Venice talks.

3. Do not do things that will make you stick out like a sore thumb.

4. When you are given work to do, settle down

and get on with it. Do not even get up in search for a rubber. Instead, cross out your mistakes.

5. If any child tries to upset you, blank it out and stay focused; or walk away from that child.

6. Reserve your play for the playground; do not play around in class.

7. Say a little prayer under your breath; ask God to help you do all these things; ask Him to let you find favour with Miss Venice.

"I will watch out for you and give you support in any way possible", I told him finally. With a smile on his face, he thanked me for the advice, and left to line up with the rest of the class.

Throughout that week, I heard no bad report about the boy. I did not see him in front of the head-teacher's office either. I then called him and asked how he was getting on. With excitement, he revealed that the things I taught him were working.

"Miss Venice has not been able to pick on me" he said, with a grin on his face.

"Praise the Lord", I said and encouraged him to continue making the effort.

"When he eventually moves on to secondary school", I thought, *"I pray he does not come in contact with another 'Miss Venice'; and if he does, may the Lord be his fortress"*. It is difficult to avoid racists, because they can be found everywhere.

What should you do as parents in situations as

these? How can you help your child? How can a child cope with racism? How can they survive in an alien environment?

HOW TO COPE WITH RACISM

1. It is of utmost importance that your child *develops and builds up self-confidence, self-esteem and dignity.* He or she needs to be strong in the Lord and in the power of His might. Any child who lacks confidence and has a low self-esteem will be crushed when faced with racist attacks. They will not be able to withstand comments passed about their background or skin colour.

Educate your child. God did not make a mistake in creating anyone black or white. God is creative and artistic. He has made people in different ways in order to add colour to the world. Use different animals, colours and surroundings as illustrations to demonstrate the unity that exists in diversity.

Look after your child very well. Make sure they eat and dress well. Engage them in hobbies that will boost their confidence. Once this is established, you have solved the problem halfway.

2. *Let your child know the meaning of racism and the evils of being a racist.* You might want to teach your child one or two things about geography and history here. Explain to him or her that people come from different backgrounds and different areas of the world. Let your child be aware that only a

small proportion of people in the world fall into the category of "racists", that they are insecure people who want to guard and protect their territory or surroundings; they do not like to share with people from other parts of the world; they are very possessive of what they think is theirs.

Encourage your child to grow a "thick skin" to empty comments from a set of ignorant people; that racist comments are not worth paying attention to. I say this because racists pass offensive comments to get you upset and angry, so much that you react and set a platform for them to get violent. It is therefore important that your child turns a deaf ear to such obscenities and not give a racist the satisfaction of carrying on with his or her plots and vendetta.

3. If racist attacks persist, encourage your child to ***alert the class teacher about what is happening.*** At the same time, your child should begin to keep a day-to-day diary of his or her experiences in the hand of child racists. Your child's diary should include

(a) Date and time.

(b) Name of child racists.

(c) The exact racist comment quoted.

(d) Witnesses.

(e) The name of the teacher your child has reported the incidence.

(f) The teacher's actions.

(g) If your child cannot read or write yet, get him

to update you about his experiences in school. If the class teacher is aware of what is happening, he or she might manage to put a stop to the racism before it gets out of hand.

4. If in spite of the teacher's awareness, the attacks worsen and nothing is done, **book an appointment to see the class teacher and voice out your concerns.** The teacher, because of your direct involvement, might take the matter more seriously and act decisively. Otherwise, take your child's diary and book another appointment to see the headteacher. Always make sure you document what was discussed and how it was followed up. Again, get to know the policy of the school about racism.

If the school has a nonchalant attitude to what is happening, it is time to move your child to another school environment. Vet thoroughly the new school before registering your child.

5. **Prayers must not stop.** Continue to pray for your child. Dedicate your child to God and mark him or her for the Lord Jesus Christ. Enlist the warring angels of God to patrol around your child constantly in Jesus' name. Immerse your child in the pool of the blood of Jesus always.

Wherever the soles of our children's feet shall touch on the face of the earth, the good Lord shall possess and give it unto them in Jesus' name. The earth is the Lord's and the fullness thereof. Where our children live, go to school, develop and grow up is their rightful garden of Eden. They have a right to cultivate, be fruitful and multiply on the land. It is a gift of life from God; they must rejoice and be glad in it.

I pray that the Lord will assassinate every serpent in our children's garden and make way for them in Jesus' name Amen. In one accord as parents, we curse everything that poses as a serpent in any area of our children's lives; we condemn such things and say they will not prosper in our children's lives in Jesus' name. Our children shall not be distracted or deceived; they shall not fall prey to oppression or intimidation; the good Lord shall raise a standard against every agenda of the evil one in Jesus name. Every weapon of racism shall not prosper in Jesus' name.

CHAPTER NINE

SATAN-PROOF ISSUES 6

SCHOOL JOURNEYS

ONCE IN a while children go out on educational trips because of a history topic, science project or religious studies. Usually, the school trip is during school hours and the children arrive back in school just before the school's closing time. Places visited include a museum, farm or even a historical church like St. Paul's Cathedral or the Norwegian Church.

The class teacher makes prior preparations for field trips. Letters are sent to parents through the children to inform them of the trip - the where, why what and when of the trip. The museum or farm will also be notified of the children's intended visit.

A teacher cannot take children out of the school premises without the company of helpers. The services of parents are sort and usually some will volunteer to come on the trip as helpers. Most day trips, if not all, are harmless. They help children see things that will compliment what they have learnt, thus enabling them to comprehend the topic better.

Occasionally, the school journey might require your child to be away for a week or weekend, to a neighbouring country, another town or for camping. This means that your child will go away with other children, the teacher and some helpers to a place you may or may not have been to before.

While most parents take things for granted, it would be wise if you ask the school a lot of questions about the school journey, the longer ones especially. Why is the school journey important? What is the purpose of the trip? How many children are going and how many adults? What are the sleeping and feeding arrangements? What kind of activities will the kids engage in? What form of transportation will they be taking? etc. Its worth asking all these questions and more before signing the parental consent form.

Make sure that the long journeys of a whole week or a weekend are not harmful to your child. You may think the school is doing you a favour by taking your child off your hands for a few days, allowing you a breathing space or overtime pay. You may also think that your child needs to have fun with his or her mates anyway. Please do not be over-assuming.

I have read in newspapers that some school journeys are cult-motivated. Some people, including teachers, who themselves are cult members, may arrange to take kids on longer school journeys to brainwash them and teach them strange doctrines while they are far from home. A lot of initiations can take place in journeys like these.

If the school journey is 'cultish' in nature, with strange activities in the night, be cautious. Children may be asked to sit in a big circle around a campfire and meditate or chant. If they are in this camp for a whole week, for instance, an innocent child might develop an interest in the things that were done there during the night.

I do not allow my children to go on school trips until I ask "thousands" of questions from the school. I also make phone calls to the camps or wherever they are going. Fortunately my children attend a Christian school and the school journeys are usually to Christian retreat centres.

My oldest daughter in secondary school went on a school journey to France. I allowed this after I had attended a parents' meeting arranged by the school to shed light on the importance and purpose of the journey. When these journeys take place, I intensify my prayers over my children.

A school journey may look innocent but you do not want to finance something that will destroy your child. If you have misgivings about any school journey, even after enquiring about it thoroughly, say "no" to the school about your child's attendance. Your child might be disappointed or even throw tantrums, but will eventually calm down. You can make it up to your child in another way. Take him to Macdonald's or buy him something he had always wanted. Just do anything other than agree to a "journey of regrets".

May the Lord protect our children from danger in Jesus' name, Amen.

SECTION THREE:

THE STRUCTURES

THE SCHOOL CURRICULUM

SPECIAL EDUCATIONAL NEEDS (SEN)

CHAPTER TEN

THE SCHOOL CURRICULUM

PLANNING

THE SCHOOL curriculum contains the programme of study compiled by the Department for Education from which each school plans what your child is required to learn. The scheme of work for each subject is then compiled by schools using the programme of study. From the scheme of work, a teacher is expected to plan the learning objectives and activities for each term in each subject.

When the termly plan is carefully tabulated and in place, a teacher then plans weekly from the termly plan. Daily lesson plans are also selected from the weekly plan for each subject. In essence, planning is narrowed down to the specifics and they focus on what the programme of study expects the children to achieve at a given period of time.

The steps followed in planning the curriculum are as follows:

1. Programme of study

2. Scheme of work

3. Termly plan

4. Weekly plan

5. Daily lesson plan

Of all these, the daily lesson plan is most detailed as it includes the learning objectives, resources, classroom organisation, introduction to the lesson, what the children will be learning, how it will be structured, any link to the other areas of the curriculum, differentiation, evaluation and follow up.

There is need to point out that the *programme of study* (compiled by the Department for Education) is the same in all schools - the same one for all state primary schools and the same for all state secondary schools. The other plans may differ, depending on the school. Each school has a structure they follow.

Every subject in the curriculum has a written policy that indicates the schools' attitude to the subject. A policy includes what the school will do in that subject and how they will carry it out.

In a nutshell, a teacher is expected, among other duties, to plan, deliver, monitor, assess, collect evidences of achievement and keep an up-to-date record of what is taught in the class.

MATERIAL RESOURCES

Resources are a crucial part of teaching and learning. Without resources little can be done or achieved. Just as a farmer needs agricultural equipments for ploughing, planting and harvesting, and a cook needs pots and pans, a school needs writing utensils, books, materials, equipment and the manpower to carry out a lot of investigative and practical tasks.

Education today is geared towards *child-centred learning strategies*. Children are provided with a lot of things to work with in order to develop a sense of reasoning and problem-tackling skills from different perspectives.

Each subject has a variety of resources it employs. In mathematics, for instance, a few of the resources are counters (for counting numbers), unifix, multilinks, weighing scales, metresticks, books, games, trundle wheels, geometry sets, etc.

HUMAN RESOURCES

Apart from material resources, the school makes use of human resources. A policeman may come into a school, for instance, and talk to children about safety and the dangers of talking to strangers. People who work in the transport sector would come to schools to talk to children about the danger of falling into train tracks. A parent may come to school to talk about the historical aspect of the environment (what it used to be).

For religious knowledge, a clergyman might visit a school to minister in the assembly; a Muslim leader may be invited to talk about Ramadhan, etc.

A parent once came to the school assembly to talk about the Chinese New Year. She explained why the Chinese named each year after a particular animal and also brought in samples of food cooked during Chinese New Year festivals. A variety of food was passed around for every child in the assembly to taste!

All resources, whether material or human, enhance the children's learning and broaden their knowledge. However, as I will explain, not all the resources used are appropriate or suitable for Christian children.

Parents who are associated with various religious festivals are often called in to talk to the children about their religion and to show them, in a practical way, examples of what they do.

One such parent visited a class during the festival of Diwali. This parent brought some sort of paint with her and drew different patterns on the palms of every child in that class. A verbal explanation about this festival would have been sufficient for the children to gain knowledge about the religion, but drawing patterns on their palms!

Another example, was a teacher who once draped herself with silver jewellery in order to teach her pupils. The topic she was treating was 'Animals' and on her jewelleries, including the rings on her fingers, was the design of different kinds of snakes.

While posters and a video are sufficient resources to teach children about 'animals', this teacher did not even stop with her weird costume. She invited a snake charmer into the classroom full of children!

The snake charmer brought about six boxes of snakes of different sizes into the classroom, and the children had to touch, feel and carry the snakes. The charmer was instructing the snakes to perform for the children and this went on all morning until lunch break. Greatly concerned, I phoned a minister who had a daughter in that class and told him to pray for his daughter that night.

From these two illustrations, you will understand why not all resources are suitable for Christian children.

Another common resource is the use of videos and television. While this is a good resource for learning, the caution is that your children might be shown programmes that you do not allow them to watch at home.

PROTECT YOUR CHILD

How can you prevent your child from being exposed to these things? How can you stop the school from involving your child in the use of unsuitable resources? One way is to book an appointment with your child's teacher and discuss at length your expectations.

Let your child's teacher understand where you stand regarding things used to illustrate learning. Explain to the teacher that you would want your child spared the exposure to things that do not glorify God. Since it does not happen all the time, your children will not miss much. Instead they will be protected against any contact with abominations.

You can also write a letter to the school authority to let them know that your child should be excused when ritual or festival foods will be tasted during the assembly. Believe me, the school will respect your wish. I know of some kids whose parents are Jehovah witnesses. These parents have written clear instructions for the school authority to follow. When we have an assembly about Jesus Christ, their children are sent out to sit in the library until assembly is over! If they see the need to "protect" their children from the truth, we should the more protect ours from error!

Some Christian parents may think this is not necessary and some may take it seriously. These examples are aimed only at making you aware of what is happening. A simpler way to avoid these things is to educate your child. If things are going on in class that do not seem right, your child can tell the teacher he would rather do something else. The teacher should respect his or her opinion.

SUBJECTS

Various subjects are taught in schools. In this section, I would like to use the primary sector as an example. Subjects that are taught mainly in primary schools are: language (literacy hour), mathematics (numeracy hour), science, design technology, information technology, history, geography, religious studies, physical education, music, art and craft.

Among these subjects, a whole hour is devoted to language and mathematics. In these two subject areas, extensive stimulating activities are set up for children to engage in and explore, after which the whole class then comes together to discuss what has been done, possible ways forward and opportunities for homework.

During literacy hour, a text is carefully chosen as the book of the week and through this text, a whole range of language areas are explored, ranging from comprehension in reading to spellings.

READING BOOKS

When was the last time you checked your child's book bag? When was the last time you assessed the books your child brings home from school? Are you too busy to bother? Watch out! Your child may be reading books that are destructive.

A book is supposed to be enjoyed. In the context of learning, it helps to improve a child's reading, recognition of words and vocabulary. A book is an inanimate teacher. From it, a child gains a lot of knowledge and information. Books supplement a child's learning by making up for what a human teacher does not cover.

All these are the attributes of a book. One afternoon, however, the Holy Spirit opened my eyes to something the devil was doing secretly.

We had just finished an interesting storybook we chose for the week and the children went for their dinner. I did not go to the staffroom because I had a lot of things to sort out in class. As I sat there pondering on where to start, suddenly the Spirit of God said to me, "Go over to the reading corner and check the books out".

I was puzzled by this instruction because I had always had a book or reading corner in my class with a variety of books - folktales, fables, fiction, non-fiction, maps, dictionaries, etc. When I heard this instruction, "Go and check the books out", I slowly got up, walked to the book corner, not knowing exactly why

I was going there. I sat down on one of the cushions and began to take the books out of the shelves. I got the shock of my life when I realised what the Holy Spirit was trying to show me. I could not believe my eyes - 90% of the books in my class were titles on witchcraft, horror, monsters and a lot of evil themes! They had always been there all the while and the children had taken them home to read! My whole body started to shake from this revelation.

The enemy we are dealing with is desperate. He is organised and has covered almost every ground, your children's school inclusive. In a subtle way, he has defiled the kiddies book market with evil. For him, it is another way of reaching innocent minds.

There are actually writers and publishers who are dedicated to publishing evil books. The school's managers, who do not know any better, will also order such books into classrooms. How organised!

God is exposing the strategies of Satan. Parents, we have no choice but to wake up! Do not go to sleep with fire on your roofs. Do not even have a nap, because it could be dangerous for your child's moral and spiritual growth.

The devil is putting financial pressures on most parents these days, forcing them to work harder to make ends meet. The few hours spent at home is barely enough to grab a bite and fall asleep. What does the devil do while parents are busy? He consistently proposes destructive ideas to children. He actively advertises his way of thinking and living through storybooks, magazines, articles, and the like.

When I saw the books in my class, I was speechless for a while. I got up, paced up and down a few times, then raced for the dustbin. I tore each book and stuffed all the shreds into the dustbin, praying all through the "clean-up operation".

After lunch, the children came in and I sat them all on the carpet. I told them my discoveries during dinner. They had never seen it that way or given it a thought. To them a book was nothing more than a book to be read. But from that day, the class was transformed. The children were careful what text they read and what to throw away.

Since that time, the first thing I do in every new class is to eliminate every inappropriate and unsuitable book from the book corner. I am careful to prevent the children from gaining access into something that will disorganise their lives.

Check the books your children are bringing home from school. Apart from this, have a discussion with them and help them realise that not all books are suitable for reading. They should not read demonic books in school or at home. There are a lot of harmless storybooks that you can obtain for your children in the shops. They do not necessarily have to be Scriptural stories. There are storybooks that would not pollute the mind of a child.

MAGAZINES

Another problem area is *magazines*. Have you been to the magazine rack of a shop lately? You will find that most of them are about horror, evil, sex, shocking fashion ideas, X-files, etc. Even kid comics are coming out with stories about revenge, destruction, and other unhealthy themes etc.

A particular ten-year-old child would rather read a magazine than do his classwork - and he did not want to be spoken to about it. Even the school authority was aware of his problem. If a teacher tried to compliment or encourage him in any way, he became violent. He did not like being told off either because when he got angry he would go all out to hurt himself. Sometimes he punched the wall so hard that his knuckles started to bleed. We were therefore asked to leave him alone.

He kept on bringing magazines about *Spiderman*, *Plasticman*, *Destroyer*, etc into the class to read and share with a small group of children he had chosen to be friendly with. The pictures and story lines in those comics were so horrifying. I wondered why any parent would buy such materials for a child who already had a problem.

As you discuss with your children, remember to caution them about the kind of materials they should not read or share with others. It may seem to be a lot of work for you as a parent, but the Holy Spirit will give you direction and grace to do it unto victory.

SCIENCE

In science, each class treats a topic either for a half term period or for a whole term, depending on the school. These science topics include discussions and investigative work. If a class has a science topic on mini-beasts, for instance, the teacher might take the children on a fieldwork to observe little insects in their natural habitat. A lot of science topics involve simple experiments that the children perform in little groups. Thereafter, they will write and share about their findings.

Some science topics and the way they are taught are in conflict with Biblical facts. They can confuse a young child who, for example, has been taught something else in Sunday school. You teach your child on Sunday that God made heaven and earth over a period of six days and rested on the seventh, and your child is told on Monday that the universe suddenly appeared through a *Big Bang*. What a confusion for a young child!

THE BIG BANG THEORY

Secular theories that deny God as the Creator, including the Darwinian evolution theory, are clearly incompatible with Bible doctrine. These same theories are tabled before your children in school.

The first question a young but curious child might ask is: *Which one is true? Did the universe burst open with a Big Bang, like a volcano eruption, or did God really create heaven and earth?*

As a Christian teacher, I have come across these kind of children who would not let go until they have clarified issues about their own existence. The very first time a child asked me for the truth, I was not sure how to deal with it, not because I do not know the truth, but because there were children from different religious backgrounds in the class at that time. As a teacher, we are not allowed to indoctrinate any pupil. So, I gave it as homework to the children to inquire if their parents believe in either the *Big Bang* or the creation of God.

At the same time, the kids were to seek their parents' consent to listen to my explanation. As soon as they came into the class the next morning, they all echoed unanimously that their parents did not mind me talking to them about God's creation from the Holy Bible.

After playtime we had science. I seized the opportunity to discuss with the children the difference between the belief of the world and Biblical belief. The children were nine and ten years old and could discern when they are being fooled, when an information is phoney, and when someone is insulting their intelligence. I picked up an encyclopaedia and asked one of the children to stand up and read the information about the 'BIG BANG' to the whole class. This is what he read:

"No-one knows why the Big Bang occurred, but scientists *think* this is what happened afterwards.

"At the moment the universe was born, it was just a minute hot ball, many times smaller than an atom. Inside was all that was needed to make the universe, though the matter and forces were unlike anything we know today. *Suddenly, it began to swell like a balloon.*

"A split second later, when it was still smaller than a football and as hot as ten billion, billion, billion °C, *gravity went mad.* Instead of pulling things together as it does now, *gravity blew the tiny universe apart, flinging it out at a fantastic rate and swelling it a thousand billion billion billion times in less than a second!* Scientists call this astonishing expansion *inflation.* Inflation provided the space for matter and energy to form" (*Children's Encyclopedia* by John Farndon, p. 78. *Emphasis mine*)

Before the child finished reading the scientists account of creation, the whole class bursted into laughter. How can a tiny little bead, grow into a balloon? How can a balloon get red with anger? How can a balloon become mad in the first place? When the balloon went mad and bursted, how could it have contained a whole universe? Do you mean the seven continents, trees, people, animals, mountains and oceans were already in that balloon? The children could not stop laughing.

I calmed them down and then pointed them to a line in the encyclopaedia where the scientist used a word of uncertainty: "The scientist *think* the universe came to be through a *Big Bang*".

"This means", I told the children, "the scientist are not sure." I went further in my explanation to what the Bible said about creation. I opened for them the Scripture that said "for lack of knowledge people perish" (Hosea 4:6), and where Jesus said "You shall know *the truth* and *the truth* shall make you free" (John 8:32).

"What is the truth?", I asked the class, and together we read the book of Genesis, chapter one: "In the beginning, God made Heaven and earth..."

At this, I stopped and told the class we would continue some other time, but they roared with excitement. They wanted more information, the whole truth; they wanted me to continue. Since we had a little bit of time before their dinnertime, I continued (Of course, I was eager to continue as they were! It was my opportunity to minister the word of God to their Word-thirsty hearts).

I explained to the children that apart from this evidence in Genesis one, that God created the Heaven and the earth in an excellent and organised way, there are other Scriptures that state that God is the Creator of the universe.

We read from Psalms 24:1-2, where it is written *"The world and all that is in it belong to the Lord; the earth and all who live on it are His"*. This first part of the passage states firmly that God owns not only the universe but also every creature in it; He created everything. The second part of the passage reveals *how* God created the universe; *"He built it on the deep waters beneath the earth, and laid its foundations in the ocean depths"*. The creation of God was very organised and systematic. It was not a disastrous *Big Bang!*

There isn't any scientist in the world, no matter their competence, knowledge or experience, who can answer God's questions in the book of Job (chapters 38-41), I told the children. God created science and the scientists. But He is the Ancient of Days; He has been before the beginning of the earth. Where was Darwin or the Darwinian theory when God created the universe? Darwin was not in existence then, so no scientist can claim to know the origin of the universe apart from the word of God.

These examples enriched the knowledge of the children about creation, they reflected and evaluated the things we discussed. I know it will go a long way with them. They are now better equipped to make up their *own* minds about which one is more logical, the *Big Bang* theory or Biblical revelation about the creation of the world.

EVOLUTION

Another science theory school children are taught is that human beings developed from apes or chimpanzees. This theory, also printed in the children's encyclopaedia, claims human beings started off looking like apes but gradually lost their hairy body, had their long hands shrink, and eventually evolved into proper human beings.

The minds of children are daily loaded with conflicting theories about life. While they need to understand the way the world thinks, children deserve to know what God has to say about issues. It is up to the Body of Christ to restructure Sunday school agendas in such a way that our children will not grow up as unbelievers (read about Sunday School in page 169).

WHO TAKES THE GLORY?

When teaching science, most teachers will magnify and glorify man's inventions and discoveries. Man-made gadgets are admired and observed by children. They are given magnets to explore electricity and kits to draw with. They are taught how to light a bulb and how to perform simple experiments. Amidst all these, they get carried away and forget that most (if not all) man-made equipment are from natural materials made by God.

God put man in charge of all the things He made. He gave us dominion over all raw materials. We take these raw materials, make them into something we need to make life comfortable for ourselves, and then we forget to acknowledge the One who provided us with the materials and the knowledge. In short, we worship the gift and not the Giver.

Children should be encouraged to appreciate God's creation around them. This is part of their spiritual development. A lot of things created by

God are used to make our own lives better. Trees are cut down everyday to make furniture, pencils, rulers, papers and doors. All these are used in school but most children are not even aware of how they are made or what they are made from. If God put a 'copyright' on all the things He made and did not give anyone the wisdom and inspiration on how to make inventions through them, the world would be a difficult place to live in.

I point out these basic things to children in my care quite often so they can have the awareness of God in all that they do; that they may have a better knowledge of how much God is involved in every aspect of their development.

God is at the centre of education. He does not want anyone to be ignorant. However, for us and our children to have a good education, God has provided an abundance of resources. A child should have an awareness of this and appreciate God for what He has done, is still doing, and will continue to do in their lives.

This, unfortunately, is not what is happening in school today. Whilst the Church is slumbering, the devil has taken over the management of schools. He has written out his own educational curriculum for schools to follow and has recruited a lot of his own followers to be teachers, thus making sure that his curriculum is well implemented. Church, it is time to rise up and fight for the future of our children.

RELIGIOUS STUDIES

Religious studies is one of the foundational subjects taught in schools. This subject is not given as much time and attention as the core subjects - Maths, English and science. Nevertheless, it is one of the subjects planned for and implemented in schools.

Because we live in a multicultural society, there are children from different religious backgrounds in every class and school. It is expected that the "Equal opportunities" policy, which is held in high esteem, is implemented in all areas of school life.

For this reason, most religious denominations and sects are taught in schools - Christianity, Sikhism, Hinduism, Buddhism, Islam, Rastafarian, etc. A teacher is expected to teach these religions and also to observe religious festivals like; Chinese new year, Festival of Light (Diwali), Halloween, Muslim idd-ul-fitr, Easter, Christmas and so on.

During a particular religious festival, there is usually a big display on the wall in an area of the school to acknowledge the religion and also an assembly for the whole school to share in the celebration of that festival. Practical aspects of the religion might be shown to the children or a leader of that religious sect might be invited to speak to children in the assembly.

At other times, a class might practise and stage a drama to show the whole school some important aspects of the religion. Some class children might make big boxes to share with the whole school how Chinese New Year is celebrated. Samples of the food eaten during celebrations might be brought into the school assembly to be shared out.

Teaching about different religions in the classroom allows children to have a knowledge of the variety of religions around them. It creates the awareness that people believe in different gods, doctrines, festivals and modes of worship.

Most parents are comfortable with their children learning about other religions other than their own. Some parents however, have problems dealing with it and want their children excused from such lessons - like the Jehovah's witness's children I mentioned earlier (page 116).

The issue of teaching a Christian child about other religions is a sensitive one. It has its advantages and disadvantages depending on how a parent perceives it. Even my opinion of this issue may conflict with the way some parents see it.

ADVANTAGES OF STUDYING OTHER RELIGIONS

For the sake of knowledge and awareness, a child who is matured may benefit from understanding a religion apart from Christianity. When a Christian child comes to a better understanding of another child's religious background, it helps the child to know why the other child dresses the way he or she does. For instance, the way Muslim children dress, especially the girls, who cover their heads for religious purposes.

The knowledge will also help a child to understand why a Muslim child would not eat bacon and sausages during dinnertime; why a Hindu child might not eat beef because a cow is a sacred animal to the Hindu religion; why a Rastafarian child has dreadlocks etc. It will in turn enlighten other children why a Christian child prays before eating his lunch in the dinner hall and so on.

Another advantage of letting a Christian child learn about other religions is that with an awareness and a background knowledge of other religions, a Christian child can be better equipped to witness to other children. If a child, for instance, enjoys witnessing, is involved in youth work or Sunday school or goes for street outreach, the knowledge about different religious practises will enhance his or her witnessing strategies. As Christian adults, God does not want us to be ignorant. He wants us to know about things going on around us. It is through knowledge that positive results can be achieved.

An ex-Muslim is more likely to win another practising Muslim for Christ because he was in that religion before he gave his life to Christ. It may take a Christian more time to achieve this, especially if the Christian does not know anything about Islam. An ex-Muslim knows what is missing in Islam and can point it out to others, using his current experiences in Christ as illustrations and testimonies. So, we see that learning about other religions has its importance.

However, I would refuse to teach other religions to the children in my class, if after assessing them, I realise they are not mature enough to cope with the differences in religion. If they are more likely to be confused or compromise their own religion, especially Christianity, I will opt out.

I have sought advise on this and have been told by the school authorities that if a group of children have a right to be excused from certain religious lessons and activities, then a teacher also has a right not to teach a variety of religions if he or she so chooses. It is therefore a flexible option for me.

My children know that listening to a teacher talk about other religions is not the danger; the danger is when they are fascinated with the religion and are drawn away from *their* faith.

The teacher of my ten year old daughter once called me to say that my daughter did not want to listen to her teach Buddhism in class. She guessed I had something to do with it. Fortunately, the teacher is an active Christian. I said to her, "if my daughter is not comfortable with the doctrines of Buddhism, she has a right to voice out her feelings".

Even at the age of ten, my daughter is old enough to decide whether she wanted to sit through a lesson on Buddhist chants or opt out.

I have books on different religions in my house, including a Koran. I have audiotapes about Jehovah's witnesses and Mormons. If the need arises, we listen to these tapes and read the books, but only for the purpose of witnessing and counselling. Other than this, I would rather go on my knees and intercede for the people involved in one religion or the other to come into the truth about Jesus Christ.

We need to pray for people in other religions, that they too will meet with Jesus who is the one and only way to the Father.

DISADVANTAGES OF STUDYING OTHER RELIGIONS

There are a couple of disadvantages in allowing a Christian child to listen to or participate in the learning of another religion.

A teacher who is involved in a religious belief will usually tend to indirectly persuade children to consider such a religion. If, by the grace of God, I was able to lead 45 children to the Lord Jesus Christ, there is no reason why a Hindu or Buddhist teacher will not try to do the same. (The parents of these 45 children all gave their consent and supported the idea of them receiving a Bible as a gift). It could also happen the other way round. May the Lord give our children the maturity, wisdom and discernment needed in situations like this. Educate and prepare your children in advance.

Another disadvantage is that some physical activities can transpire during the lesson, which may result in negative spiritual contacts for your child (eg.

eating foods sacrificed to idols mentioned earlier). A teacher can invite a mother to show the class in a practical way how things are done in her religion. The mother, wanting to impress the class, may bring food or incense to the class, or teach them how to chant. This is where a line should be drawn. God does not want us or our children to partake in evil feasts or lifeless rituals.

You alone can decide what your son or daughter participates in with respect to religion. Visit the headteacher or your child's teacher and have a friendly, informal chat about the school's attitude to religion and festivals. Learn how far the school would go to demonstrate the activities of a particular religion to the children.

Let the school authority and your child's teacher know the extent to which you will allow your child to participate in such learning activities. If possible, back this up with a letter for record purposes. As much as possible, make it your business to know the topics in religion that would be treated, so you can have a prior knowledge of what might be done in that during the lesson.

The most important thing to do is to enlighten your children. Educate them on the pros and cons of religion so that they can know what to do during the extreme cases.

Do not wait until your children are asked to make costumes or disguises for Halloween before you act. Halloween, the annual festival for witches, is a big celebration in the western world. There is scarcely any shop you go to during Halloween celebration without life-size models of witches flying on brooms. In classrooms, children are asked to make models of witch's costumes - pumpkins, hats, broomsticks - or they write a spooky story to celebrate Halloween. May the good Lord deliver our children from all evil learning objectives.

I once taught a class of nine year olds, starting from the first half of the autumn term. By the end of the second half of the spring term, they had learnt, for their age, enough about the word of God to help them discern between right and wrong.

At one point, I had to go off-sick for three days during which a supply teacher covered my class. When I resumed back in school, my pupils told me they did not like the supply teacher at all.

"Why did you not like her", I asked.

"She dressed in a spooky way", they told me. "She talked like a witch, yelled and screamed at us".

They then went ahead to show me a copy of the worksheet she gave them during religious studies. It was a word search - one with a difference. On the word search was everything to do with evil. A few examples of words the kids were supposed to search for were "sorcery", "witchcraft", "black cat", "wizard", "devil", "Lucifer", "Halloween", "blood", "coven" and many other weird words.

"When we refused to do it", the children

continued, "she yelled at us and threatened to report us to the head teacher". They were forced to participate in the evil game.

During playtime, they all squeezed the paper into their pockets and threw them away. They were wise enough to keep one for me to see so that I could believe what they had to tell me.

They now understood why I talked to them about the Word of God. They told me that when they saw the teacher, they started to plead the blood of Jesus under their breath!

Appreciate the importance of teaching your children the principles of God's Word. It is a disaster to fall prey into the hands of the devil. We parents have a lot of work to do and I know that the Holy Spirit will help us to fulfil our spiritual duties over our children.

CHAPTER ELEVEN

SPECIAL EDUCATIONAL NEEDS (SEN)

THERE ARE groups of children who come under a special category called *Special Educational Needs (SEN)*. Some children are categorised as needing *special* education because they:

1. have learning difficulties

2. have behaviour problems

3. have physical disabilities

Added to the list is many, if not all, bilingual children. Special needs children could also be gifted and intelligent children who are working above the level of their age groups.

Children who fall under the SEN grouping have specially trained classroom assistants who work with them inside, or sometimes outside the classroom set-up. Under normal circumstances they work within the classroom.

Some SEN children who have severe behavioural problems are assigned individual helpers who work with them. A lot of time and attention is given to these children than to those who require special education because they are gifted. The gifted ones are automatically expected to be stimulated and challenged in differrent subject areas. Unfortunately, this is not always the case, because the activities in the class, especially subject-based tasks, which are usually simplified for SEN children, become too simple for them.

For example, if the whole class is working out some long multiplication sums, the struggling ones might be expected to work on basic multiplication facts using practical means like counting unifix or multilinks (plastic cubes used in counting numbers). Again, if some children are asked to make sentences, the struggling ones might be expected to work on a simple spelling pattern like: *all, call, fall, gall, wall* and so on.

Most bilingual children fall into the category of SEN because of their difficulty in speaking fluent English or understanding English words for objects. They may well be clever children, but their language problem, which is not their fault, restricts them to the SEN grouping.

HOW ARE SEN CHILDREN REGISTERED?

How do children get registered for special needs? When a teacher is concerned about a child's level of achievement or a child's behaviour, the concern is registered with the school head teacher. The child's progress is then monitored over a period of time. If there is no improvement, a letter is sent to the child's parents, asking them to see the class teacher.

A meeting is held with the parents and a way forward is discussed and outlayed. The recommendations from the meeting is then reviewed at a later stage. If there is still no improvement, the parents are advised that their child needs extra help. The advise given at this stage is the addition of the child's name to the list of special needs children. The parents are told that this would ensure that the school gets the help they need for the child.

Sometimes, educational psychologists are involved in this process. When the process is complete, a SEN file is opened for the child which will contain detailed paper work about the needs and progress of the child. The same process goes for a child with behaviour problems.

AN EVIL MARK

I do not want to go into the nitty-gritty of what is involved in SEN other than let you know that in some instances, it is a blemishing mark on a child's record. On the surface, the idea of separating some children as SEN is good, but in many respects, it serves as an evil register for labeling some children as abnormal.

As a parent, you need to prayerfully get your child's name off the SEN list. Once an SEN file is open for your child, it remains as a point of reference in the future.

One of my daughters was tagged SEN not because of learning problems, but because she had severe eczema that made her itch and cry in the classroom when she was uncomfortable. Our consent as parents was not sought before her name was registered as SEN. We did not even know who carried out the assessment of her situation.

She was put on stage three of special needs straight away (Stage three indicates a severe problem of SEN and the severity increases with every stage, the highest being five). I fought against this for many years, especially that it was done without any signature from my husband or myself.

At one point, I went to the office of the head teacher to plead with her, 'mother to mother'. She said to me that my daughter could not come off that register until a review was done. Even after my daughter got a lot better from the eczema and stopped itching and crying, the school still refused to take her name off the SEN list.

I went back to the headteacher again, this time with determination. I did not plead with her but said emphatically, "I must not see "S.E.N. stage 3" written on my daughter's school report again. I do not want her showing such a report at secondary school interviews".

I firmly told the head teacher that I was ready to

seek legal advice and consult the education department if the SEN category appeared on my daughter's school report again. And I meant it.

Meanwhile, I went into spiritual warfare about the matter. The next time I attended the parents evening to see my daughter's school report, the first place I checked was the SEN line. Instead of "SEN stage 3", they simply wrote "N/A" meaning "Not Applicable"! To God be glory for this victory.

GHOST REGISTER

The SEN register is not only an evil register and an evil mark but also a money making scheme for schools. Most of the time, the number of children put on the SEN register do not need to be there at all. However, since each child registered as SEN fetches the school some money from the government, schools try to include as many children as possible, tagging them as hopeless or write-off cases.

The head teacher of one school told a teacher one day, "I have included two children's names in your class register and have enlisted them as SEN children".

"When are they resuming class", the teacher asked curiously.

"Do not worry", the head teacher said, smiling. "They do not exist. They are imaginary children and will fetch the school nothing less than a thousand pounds each".

"Really?", asked the teacher, who could not hide her surprise at this revelation.

No wonder why school's will refuse to take a child's name off the SEN register - it boosts the school's economy.

A CRUDE BUSINESS VENTURE

A nine-year-old Nigerian boy transferred from another school to my class. He started at the beginning of the spring term. Two weeks into the term, the head teacher asked me how the boy was getting on. I told her that he was settling in well, working hard, was a good reader and very well behaved. The head teacher was shocked. She did not believe me.

She explained to me why she was shocked. Apparently, a very fat file on the case of this boy was sent to our school from the previous school. In this robust file, it was stated that the boy had speech problems and was undergoing fifteen hours of speech therapy every week. It was also documented that he was a slow learner and hyperactive.

Well, I brought out the work he did for two weeks and later in the afternoon, made him read a level three book to the head teacher. Obviously, in his previous school, they had thoroughly used him as a business venture and he had yielded big financial interests for his school!

The cycle was going to repeat itself in spite of the evidence I gave to the head teacher of the boy's potential. An Educational Psychologist and Speech Therapist was assigned to observe the boy in my class. She came with a pad and a pen, monitored the boy around the class and kept on 'penning away'.

At the end of the class, the therapist said that the boy needed more hours of help. When I asked her the reasons why, she came out with a lot of jargon. If the boy needed all the abbreviations the psychologists poured out, I would not have raised any question.

I could see the motives of the psychologist and the school. She wanted to keep her job and the head teacher wanted to boost her school's pocket.

I invited the boy's mother to come and see me and explained what was going on to her.

"Why did you sign your child to the SEN group?", I asked her.

"I thought the school was genuinely helping him", she said.

"Has your boy ever developed speech problems?", I asked, wanting to get to the root of this issue.

"No", she answered.

"Why on earth did he have to undergo speech therapy?"

"Because his teacher at that time said he was too quiet", said the mum.

I cried out in surprise, "Is it a sin to be quiet!".

I was sorry for the boy and the mum. She had allowed this to go on for too long. By the time she started to fight the authorities, it was too late. They threatened to report her to the social services if she continued to "interfere" with the boys learning programme.

I advised both mum and child to find yet another school for her child, where the boy's potential will be realised. The plan was not to let the school know about the change so that the evil file would not follow him to the new school.

She found a new school for the boy in another Borough but because the former school kept phoning her for the address of the new school, she had no choice but to send her boy to a boarding school in Nigeria. A year later, she called me and testified that her child's school report was excellent - he was top in his class! Praise God!

WE CAN HELP

God has helped me to pull other children out of this miry clay - children who have been written off like the boy above. *"All good gifts come from heaven"*. God does not make mistakes. Children are gifts and they are intelligent. God did not accidentally pour 'runny custard' into anyone's brain.

There are, indeed, children who need genuine help with learning and behaviour problems. There are those who need our prayers for healing. But we need to dig deep into the foundation of why a child is the way he or she is, and not turn them into money-making ventures. Through prayer and effort we can help these children realise their potentials.

I have proof of what the power of God can do in children's lives. They do not deserve to be 'written off'. Their problems should not be commercialised or turned into profits. I fervently believe that there is a development programme that will work for individual children that need special attention.

Another six year-old girl that I met in the supplementary school I taught in, was tagged a SEN child. Whenever she came to the Saturday school, she would shed big tears because she was scared of working. We used to call her 'raindrops', unaware of what she was going through.

Her dad got very concerned and arranged for her to see me for help. Before I took her on, I asked her dad a bit of her background and why she hated studying. Her dad told me that he did not have any patience with her. He would usually get upset and smack her whenever she got a sum or spelling wrong. He did this also because he was not happy that she was categorised as SEN in her school. This information helped me to approach the girl strategically.

For the first two weeks, I did not teach her directly, rather I spoke to her and chatted with her. My aim was to help her relax and trust me. By the third week, I slowly introduced her to paper and pencil through playing games. She did not know that learning could be fun! She soon settled down to work and to the glory of God the Father, the girl learnt to read in two weeks! This is another successful case by God's grace.

WHAT DO YOU SEE IN YOUR CHILD?

Have you experienced any of these SEN nightmares? Is your child categorised as a hopeless case? Are you worried? Have you lost hope? Do you believe the school's report? In the light of the information you have received, please think again.

Call your child and have a proper look at him or her. What do you see in your child? Can't you see the genius in your child? Is he or she not a clever, brilliant and intelligent child? If you believe in the uniqueness of your child, you have to cancel all the negative emblems the devil is trying to stick on him or her. Do not accept the SEN tag. Accept God's opinion instead. Speak normality and success into every cell in your child's system.

PRAY! PRAY!! PRAY!!!

Pray for your children consistently and ward off every evil spirit that wants to attach itself to them from their early years.

My children can do all things through Christ who loves them. God says that my children shall be tops not tails. God says it is well with them. My children are more than

conquerors *through Christ Jesus who strengthens them.*
They overcome evil, hopelessness and failure through the
blood of the lamb and through the word of their testimony.

My children shall be taught of the Lord and great shall
be their peace. They shall be more knowledgeable than
their teachers and contemporaries. God has not given my
children the spirit of fear, timidity or failure, but God has
given them the power to succeed, excel and increase.

God is the only one who knows the plan that He has for
my children. It is not a plan of failure or hopelessness; it is
a plan to enable them to accomplish the purpose of God for
their lives. I refuse to see my children from the worldly
point of view, or from the school's point of view. Every
negative opinion of my children is cancelled in Jesus'
name. I disconnect my children from every evil
entanglement. I cut them off from every evil soul tie. I
release their knowledge ability from bondage, and plug
them to the power source of the Holy Ghost. It is well with
my children for they are children of God...

Pray! Pray!! Pray!!! Do not allow the devil to
harass you with fear or lies.

GET THEIR NAME OFF THE REGISTER

Do not stop praying for any of your children
registered as an SEN pupil. At the same time, make it
a goal to get his or her name off the register -
whatever its going to cost you. Make it a point of
duty to monitor your child's school work. If you are
not satisfied with the performance, find time to

supplement his or her learning. You can enrol your child in a Saturday school, arrange for private home tuition or teach him yourself. As your child improves, get the school to do a performance review and make sure that he or she continues to climb up the ladder of achievement.

Insist that the school strikes off the name of your child from their SEN register. Otherwise, it is time for you enrol your child in another school—where your child will be celebrated rather than tolerated.

If any of your children *genuinely* needs extra help, God will make His healing power available for him or her*. He can deliver anyone from the bondage of learning difficulties. Minister in prayer constantly to them, and confess the word of life into them everyday. We serve a God who answers prayers by fire; the Lord God of Hosts is a Deliverer.

There is nothing difficult for Him to do. He will resuscitate every cell that your child needs to stimulate his learning process in Jesus name. There is nothing hard for our God to do. Remember, He created them, knows them and loves them.

---

*I believe that there are effective programmes that can help genuine SEN children. A detailed treatment of such programmes is beyond the scope and purpose of this book

SECTION FOUR:

THE SOLUTIONS

DO THESE STRATEGIES WORK?
- CHRISTIAN SCHOOLS?
- PRIVATE SCHOOLS?
- OVERSEAS SCHOOLS?

PARENTAL RESPONSIBLITIES

CHURCH RESPONSIBILITIES

CHAPTER TWELVE

DO THESE STRATEGIES WORK?

NOW THAT all this information has been revealed, what can we do as parents? Surely, we do not want our children polluted by the world and yet they have to learn, work and live among others in this world.

How can we make sure our children remain stable in an unstable world? How can our children retain their peace in a war-torn world? What can we do to make sure that our children survive in an alien environment? How can we obtain a well-balanced education that glorifies God for our children? How can our children keep their heads where others are loosing theirs? Will a Christian school solve the problem? Will private education get us the answer?

A lot of questions need answers in the light of the truths outlayed. All of them are urgent issues. As a matter of fact, the educational system is in a state of emergency. It cannot be ignored any longer.

IT SHOULD BE SAFE HERE

A lot of parents have withdrawn their children from state schools to seek solace in schools set up by orthodox churches (for example, Catholic schools and Church of England Schools - C.E). Some on the other hand have registered their children into private schools where they pay school fees. Yet, others have sent their children to their country of origin hoping for a miracle.

The question now is whether these alternatives solve the problem plaguing the educational system of this nation. It may shock you to know that none of them is guaranteed to help *your* child on the long-run.

CHRISTIAN SCHOOLS?

A lot of so-called "Christian schools" have compromised Christian values and principles for various reasons. They still have to plan and implement the government's programme of study and teach a variety of stuff to children that is not suitable. Moreover, you will find in a Christian school, teachers that are not Christians or those who bear the name "Christian" but do not fully comprehend or live by spiritual principles.

These "Christian schools" also register kids from other religions and therefore, have no choice but to implement the Equal Opportunities policy. Consequently, nothing much changes when you withdraw a child from a state school and register him in a

Church or Christian school.

A lot of parents who are not Christian pretend to be in order to get their children a place in a Christian school. Some religiously attend Catholic Churches and go as far as being confirmed or baptised just to get their children into a Catholic school. Once their children are registered in the school, these parents go to Church a few more times and then withdraw from Church. To them, they have accomplished their mission. They are not Christians at all but are desperate enough to do anything to get their children registered in a Christian school. They assume that their kids will get a better deal of education in a Christian school environment.

What much of Christianity is left in such schools where admission is through deception? Most of the kids of these non-Christian parents are also not Christian. They will bring with them a lot of worldly ideas with which they can influence a Christian child. At the end of the day, an establishment like this is just another state school in disguise.

PRIVATE SCHOOLS?

What about private schools? A private school in conjunction with a Church tends to have few children and the classrooms are not crowded. In such schools, a teacher has a better chance of being able to stimulate the children in their learning. The teacher is able to have a better control over the class and possibly able to give individual children the support they need in any area of their learning.

There are few children in a private school because not many parents can afford to pay the school fees private schools charge.

It is great if a school is private and Christ-centred. The children are more likely to have a balanced child-development programme with high moral standards. The awareness of Christ will also be built into the everyday activity of the school. The children would literally feel the peace of Christ in their environment. There would be an all-round calmness in the school.

Private Christian schools have a chance of maintaining a good educational standard if they will not compromise their God-given vision because of financial hardships. Inability to pay bills, keep staff and maintain the building will force a private school to either close down or bend to the way of the world in some way or another.

Some Christian establishments have even been known to apply for lottery grants or play syndicate lottery for funds. If this is happening, the probability that the school will end up becoming another state school in disguise exists.

OVERSEAS SCHOOLS?

Parents who send their children thousands of miles away to their country of origin do so in search for a better education.   I pray that they get their heart's desire. Some parents achieve their goal while others have regretted their decision.

Whatever the reason why parents choose this option for their children, they also have to bear the cost involved. When a child is sent abroad to study, the parents have to send money not only for school fees, but also for maintaining the child. They also have to respond to every demand from their children's guardian.

Sometimes, money sent home may not be used for the purpose for which it is sent. At the end of the day, the fortune invested is not guaranteed to yield any interest.   Many parents who send children abroad end up bringing them back to the UK to continue their studies.

Apart from cost, some children have been initiated into witchcraft because the guardians they stayed with are members of covens.   Anything can happen to a child who is not directly under the parent's care.

A young girl was sent home by her parents to continue schooling in Nigeria. She stayed with her grandmother and her parents dutifully transfered money for her upkeep. Because the grandmother loved the girl so much, she initiated her into witchcraft. By the time the girl came back to UK, she was worse than when she left to Nigeria.

Unless in situations beyond a parent's control, I

believe parents should directly take care of their children. It is easier to monitor their development this way. If God has given us children, they are our personal responsibility and not the responsibility of somebody else.

So, these three options are not long-term solutions of the nationwide educational problem. What then, must we do to permanently *Satan-Proof* our children? Surely there must be a way.

CHAPTER THIRTEEN

PARENTAL RESPONSIBILITES

O UR CHILDREN are expecting us to wake up and do something. But what can we do to ensure a healthy moral development for them? How can we stop the devil in his tracks as he attempts to influence innocent children through loopholes in the existing educational system?

CHARITY BEGINS AT HOME:
A PARABLE OF A CHILD'S GROWTH

Moral and spiritual growth begins at home. Therefore, the foundation of a child's life must be ploughed with prayer, love and sensitivity by parents in the home setting.

The seeds of moral and spiritual development should find root very early in a child's life. Parents, thereafter, have the responsibility of observing the growth of these seeds. On a regular basis, they will have to tend, nurture and water these seeds through God's Word, fervent prayers, discipline and love.

The growth of children at home is so important. It requires close monitoring everyday.

As the roots of morality and godly principles become strong in the heart of a child, it will start to shoot out as character. These tender buds must then be directed towards the sunlight of the glory of God where they can be fed with the life-giving power of God.

Where can you expose your child to the "sunlight" that emanates from God? In the gathering of the saints! Take your children to Church regularly where they can hear God's Word and learn God's ways. Encourage them to read a portion of the word of God everyday. Pray *for* and *with* them. Minister to them and let them minister to you. Expose them to spiritual disciplines that will help them grow in the things of God.

SPARE NOT THE ROD

As they grow, it is also important that you prune them of any weed that will try to attach itself to their character. Weeds choke life out of plants, especially young plants. They also hinder the future growth of healthy leaves. Cut off immediately every "weed" that manifests in your child's life. The Bible encourages us to do so.

> *"Children just naturally do silly, careless things* **but a good spanking will teach them how to behave"** *(Pr 22:15 GNB).*

"Discipline your children while they are young enough to learn. If you don't, you are helping them to destroy themselves" (Pr 19:18 GNB).

"Correction and discipline are good for children. *If they have their own way, they will make their mothers ashamed of them"* (Pr 29:15 GNB).

Children cannot help being children at times. This is why "pruning" is necessary. It does not mean that you should beat your child physically all the time, though. Some parents are "cane-fingered". At the slightest misbehaviour, the cane shows up!

Spanking is an idiomatic expression. It can be done through words or through a withdrawal of privileges that a child enjoys. For the purpose of correcting a wrong footing, you can deny your child something dear to him or her, and then reinstate the privilege when the correction is established. If at every opportunity you beat your children, they will grow a thick skin to the beating and the discipline will not have the desired effect in them any longer.

As a child, I lived with my big aunt who was quick to use the cane. Her punishment was always heavier than the crime. I was beaten so often that eventually I became immune and numb to the "torture". If you are like my aunt, be careful; your spanking will soon lose its effect and your child might grow hatred and bitterness in his or her heart for you.

I have heard some children in school say, "I cannot wait until my 16th birthday to leave home". Physical spanking should be a last resort. By the time you decide to use the cane, your child would realise that he or she has gone too far.

GODLY DISCIPLINE

Remember the Scriptural admonition in Ephesians 6:4: *"Parents, do not treat your children in such a way as to make them angry, instead bring them up with Christian discipline and instruction" (GNB).* How can this be achieved?

Every child, I believe can be *spoken* to in a loving and intelligent manner. A discussion with a child who has made a mistake is the first step in the process of correction.

Give your children a chance to reflect on what they do wrong. The need for them to understand step by step where a mistake lies, how they have gone off the track, is important. They need to know through discussion the reasons and implications of their unacceptable actions.

They also need to understand your expectations and more importantly, God's expectations for them. You can counsel your own children because you are qualified through God (and responsible) to do so.

Some kids do not need a war of words; they would rather have you to be constructive with them. They need you to structure their characters lovingly and carefully.

Children also need a *role model*. You are the closest example that they can imitate. Let your lifestyle be an example to them. Be your children's role model. Jesus is our ultimate model. As you fashion your life in conformity to Christ, your children will copy you. If you pray, they will pray. If you go to Church, they will follow you. If, on the other hand, you indulge in lies, be sure that they will grow up as liars.

ACT WHILE THEY ARE YOUNG

Your child needs you to trim off every branch of unwanted behaviour using shears of love and tenderness. Do so early in their life. Do not wait until they get out of hand. Correcting children when they are older is harder and painstaking than when they are young. A plant that is not tended, watered and nurtured will dry up and die. In the process of drying up all sorts of pests and creepy reptiles will speed up the destruction process of that plant.

If a child lacks moral and spiritual development, he or she will be surrounded by destructive ideas from peer groups, media, environment, etc. "Where there is a dead body, vultures will gather", the Bible says. It takes God's grace and wisdom to replace these ideas with God's principles when they are old.

SPEND TIME WITH YOUR CHILDREN

Spend quality time with your children. Time invested into their lives is more valuable than the income gained from working extra hours. Some kids, especially the older ones, claim that their parents do not know or understand them. You cannot understand your children if you do not spend time with them.

Your children are unique individuals with distinct personalities. Get to know each of them by spending time with them - one by one. This way, you will know what to encourage and what to discourage in their behaviour.

Set apart a family time that will be your special time with the children. Engage them in fruitful and rewarding hobbies rather than leave them idle. *"The devil finds work for idle hands"*. Do not leave them to roam on the street all the time. There are a lot of extra-curricular activities children can do, which will take their minds off pranks and mischief. They can learn to play a musical instrument, participate in sports (e.g. swimming, athletics etc.), join homework clubs, visit the library and so on.

MORE EDIFYING ACTIVITIES

Create a *prayer room* or a prayer area in your home where you can minister to your family, especially the children.

Encourage your children to *read* a variety of

Christian literature, *listen* to audiotapes, and *watch* Christian videos or the Christian Channel. Do this together with them from time to time.

Give your children *spiritual responsibilities* at home. Rotate family Bible studies. Have a rota for family prayer meetings. This way, your children will grow and flourish in the things of God.

Find time to *go out with your children*, probably on a stroll, where you can all admire the beauty of God in nature. *Explore the environment* together. Through this, you will encourage prayer-walking. Do all these in a relaxed and informal way. This will strengthen your relationship with your children and at the same time build them up in Christ.

START EARLY! START NOW!

Christian parents raising children in the western society need to work hard at developing Bible-based morals in their children. The devil is all out to destroy the lives of kids, but if we stand up against him, he will flee. The key word for parents is: *Start early; Start now!* Tomorrow may be too late.

Do not wait for more convinient circumstances before you take up your responsibility over your children. Create time for them. Engage in spiritual warfare on their behalf. Have a vision of victory for them. By all means, *Satan-proof your children!*

A PRAYER

Lord Jesus, give me the grace, strength and wisdom I need to bring up my children in the ways of the Lord. Protect them from the onslaughts of Satan at school, home and wherever they go. Let my boys grow up to be the Samuels of their generation. Let my girls grow to be the Deborahs of their generation. They will not fall. They will not stumble. They will impact the world with the life and love of Jesus Christ. They will not depart from the faith, but will remain steadfast, rooted and grounded until the second coming of the Lord. I and the children you have given unto me, we are for signs and wonders in the land. My children are like arrows in the hand of a mighty man. They are like battle axes in Your hand. Use them for your glory. May they influence other children for you. The world will not pollute them. Sin will not entice them. You will keep them safe, now and forever.

Thank you Jesus! Amen.

CHAPTER FOURTEEN

CHURCH RESPONSIBILITIES

A NON-NEGOTIABLE CHRISTIAN EDUCATION

OUR CHILDREN need an environment condu-
cive for the anointing of God to learn. Evidently, this
is not achievable within the present educational
structure. Is it not time for the Body of Christ to snap
out of slumber and pray earnestly for the establishment of Christ-centered schools all over the nation?

There is no better solution to the problem of our
children's educational predicament: *Believers must
rise with a vision to insure the future of our children
with God-directed learning.* This option is non-
negotiable. Are we not concerned about the tactics of
Satan against the next generation of Christians?

HINDERANCES

There are two major strategies, amongst many
others, that the devil is using to prevent Christians
from embarking on the "rebuilding" of the ruined

educational walls. Just as Tobias and Sanballat rose against Nehemiah and the Jews who were rebuilding the walls of Jerusalem, Satan is bent on frustrating any effort to establish non-compromising Christian schools in our communities.

Finance

The Church is overdue for a financial breakthrough. The plight of private Christian schools has been to beg for crumbs under the table of the prince of this world, hence compromising spiritual principles. When Christ-centred schools seek for financial support from non-Christian bodies, there are conditions that have to be met. "We will support you if...".

Let us trust God for the removal of every financial constraint that hinders the Church. We need the wisdom and anointing of God where money is concerned.

Disunity

The second and probably most effective strategy of Satan against the Church is disunity. There is a serious case of division in the Church today that hinders progress and growth. Even when someone rises up with a vision to start a Christian school, the force of disunity acts against the vision.

> *"Every kingdom divided against itself is brought to desolation; and every city or house divided against itself shall not stand"* (Matt 12:25).

No matter the name of the ministry, where it is

located and what it does, we are one Body. Ministry names are for identification purposes. The Body of Christ can join forces together with a vision to launch centres of learning that will serve the educational needs of our children.

The Church, like our physical body, has been put together by God to work in unity.

> *"For the body itself is not made up only of one part, but of many parts. If the foot were to say, 'Because I am not a hand, I don't belong to the body,' that would not keep it from being a part of the body. And if the ear were to say, 'Because I am not an eye, I don't belong to the body,' that would not keep it from being a part of the body. If the whole body were just an eye, how could it hear? And if it were only an ear, how could it smell? As it is, however, God put every different part in the body just as he wanted it to be. There would not be a body if it were all only one part!* **As it is, there are many parts but one body.** *So then, the eye cannot say to the hand, 'I don't need you!' Nor can the head say to the feet, 'Well, I don't need you!'" (1 Cor 12:14-21 GNB).*

If ministries continue to do their own things in their own little corners, outshining each other with colourful fliers and programmes, the crucial things that need to be done in the society will not be accomplished. Whether a ministry is big or small, famous or has never been heard of, is irrelevant. What matters is that Churches and Ministries should destroy the walls of demarcation, break every barrier and partition, get together and help one another.

> *"And so there is no division in the body, but all its different parts have the same concern for one another. If one part of the body suffers, all the other parts suffer with it; if one part is praised, all the other parts share its happiness"* (1 Cor 12:25,26 GNB).

When ministries come together in one accord, they can pull resources together and propel the vision of proper Christian schools that will not condescend to the world's mode of operation.

Muslims have Islamic schools and they will not compromise their standards. I doubt if you will find a single Christian child in an Islamic set up. While I am not advocating that non-Christians cannot attend a Christian school (after all, our aim is to populate the kingdom of Heaven and spread the knowledge of Christ's glory), the point is that we need non-compromising Christian schools, and it would take the whole Church to team up for a successful and effective venture.

THE TIME IS *NOW!*

There is no better time to run with a vision for Christian education than now. The world's system is not going to get better. The devil will continue to manipulate and explore the system to meet his own ends. The time to act is *now*. We cannot wait until Satan completely ruins the lives of innocent children.

A balanced Christian education will focus on the all-round growth of children. It would offer counselling sessions to both parents and children that arc registered in the school. All school activities, including the curriculum, will be designed with Jesus at the centre. Without Christ, things fall apart.

A lot of bad things are happening in the world of today. We can no longer stand aside and allow our children to partake of them. Church, we need to come together and stop competing against each other. It is time for us to re-experience the book of Acts. For the sake of our children, we must come together, give what we have and be part of the vision of establishing schools with a difference - schools that even the people of the world will see as role model and change their ways.

Finance must not be a barrier to what God wants to do. Doctrinal differences should not hinder either. Together we can bring this vision into reality and build something our children will live to thank us and glorify God for.

SUNDAY SCHOOL

Sunday schools play an important role in the moral and spiritual development of children. They are "gap bridgers" where education is concerned. The state schools provide academic learning while the Sunday school fills in the blanks with moral and spiritual learning.

Academic development or achievement does not make a complete child. A child who develops academic skills but lacks good morals will grow to become an outward academic giant, and an inward spiritual dwarf - like an attractive car without an engine to propel it torwards a specific direction.

There is a limit to what academic achievement can do. It cannot sustain or preserve one during trials, temptations, and the challenges of life. They will not be sufficient for making decisions that affect daily living. There are a lot of PhD. holders today who have no moral values and lack spiritual under-standing. Because they only have their academic theories to rely upon in life, they soon find out that academic prowess does not always impart wisdom; it does not equal maturity. What gives a man wisdom and maturity is reverence for the Lord, and this is acquired through moral and spiritual instruction.

Whilst the schools are busy concentrating on raising standards of achievement in academics, the Body of Christ must begin to nurture children morally and spiritually. This is why Sunday schools need restructuring today.

Sunday schools should no longer be used as crèches where children are kept quiet so they do not disturb the adult Church. They are not play groups where children are gathered and fed with biscuits and drink to keep them from disturbing their parents during the sermon.

The Sunday school curriculum must cover the areas of a child's development that are overlooked by the schools. For effectiveness, it is important that children are grouped into different age groups. Each age group should have a programme of spiritual development suitable for the group.

Five year olds may learn about the love of Jesus, for instance, sing and clap their hands, while the twelve year olds may find the approach to the session boring. When Sunday schools are structured as classrooms and the word of God is the subject, it is not possible to teach a subject at the same level to a five and twelve year old.

Churches must at this time invest sizeable amounts of money for the development of the Children's Church. The Sunday School should not be the last item on the budget allocation list. In the light of the things uncovered in this book, a renewed dedication to improving the Sunday School is important.

ADVISE FOR SUNDAY SCHOOL WORKERS

Sunday school teachers and co-ordinators have a delicate task to carry out because they work with children every week. There are a lot of children from different backgrounds and different situations to cope with. Their jobs are of a different nature from that of adult pastors.

Whereas most adults are set in their ways, children are receptive, their hearts are tender and they are in the formative part of their lives. Because of this, the children's pastor needs *extra wisdom* from above and *sharp discernment* of the Holy Ghost to have a breakthrough with each individual child.

As a children's Church minister, you are also *accountable* to God about the part you play in shaping the life of each child you work with. You cannot afford to take your responsibilities lightly.

You should intercede always for each child in your care. Your job satisfaction and success will depend on the strength of your relationship with God. He will give you instructions and strategies to work with each child if you ask Him

When any of the kids in your class do not turn up in Church, ***you should work hard to find them, follow them up and bring them back into the sheepfold.*** If anyone of them is wounded or hurt, you must ask God to use you as a balm for their healing.

Work together with parents. Give them reports on the progress of their children. Solicit their cooperation. Encourage them to devote time to the children at home; to help with home work and Bible reading and prayer.

Consider your class a place where young soldiers for Christ are raised. It is not a playground or creche. Do not constipate the children with biscuits and fizzy drinks. ***Nourish them with the word of God.***

Children will cope better with the problems they face in school if thcy are adequalely prepared for battle in their spiritual school - the Sunday school. As they grow in their knowledge of God's Word, they will have a better understanding of what is going on around them.

A THREE-FOLD CORD

A three-fold cord is not easily broken. If these three strategic areas are adequately taken care of, that is, training at home by parents, a conducive learning environment created by the establishent of Christian schools and a well-structured Sunday School in the Church, our children will be safe from Satan's wicked onslaughts. They will stand the test of time and eternity. They will be better equipped to affect their generation for Jesus Christ.

CONCLUSION

THE STANDARD of education our children are getting today is well below the standard of some decades ago. It is my prayer that the Almighty God will use this book to stir up effective prayer for children in the Body of Christ. Can you compare the learning environment you grew up in with the environment of today?

The things that would have been an abomination in those days are now the very things in vogue. Who would ever have thought that homosexuality would become a subject good enough to be taught in schools? Why is it that children are allowed to dress anyhow to school these days?

In those days, there was a balanced, all round education, academically, morally and spiritually. In our day and age, morals have been reduced to nothing and spirituality stumped out of the classrooms. As Christian parents, we cannot pretend not to see what is going on around us. God knows why He commanded us to bring up our children in His way. The command is still valid in this electronic and computer age.

> *"Never forget these commands that I am giving you today, teach them to your children. Repeat them when you are at home and when you are away, when you are resting and when you are working" (Deut 6:6,7).*

If you teach your children, the Bible says that *"everything would go well with you and your descendants forever"* (Deut 5:29b).

Children are not too young to be rooted in the things of God. Many young people have been called and used by God in the past. Joseph was young when he represented God in Egypt. He did not yield to the temptation of Potipher's wife. David had confidence in the Lord as a lad, and was able to slay Goliath and bring glory to God.

The Lord who did it in Biblical times can do it in our time. He can use our children for great things. Our children must not tap-dance to the jungle music of this world. There is a heavenly agenda they must follow. We have the responsibility of guiding them through it by the help of the Holy Spirit.

We need to prayerfully rewind and erase with the blood of Jesus, all worldly programmes that have been recorded on the "tape" of our children's lives. We then have to "record" God's kingdom principles of truth into them.

If there is any way we have been negligent in the past, let us repent wholeheartedly and God will forgive. May God give to us the wisdom to make amends before the situation is out of hand.

When you dress your child up for school in the morning, always remember this fact: *Your child's school has become a battleground of life.* Therefore, do not just help your child wear his or her school uniform, but also the whole armour of God.

Never let your children (big or small) step out of the house in the morning without drenching in the blood of Jesus Christ. They are soldiers of Christ and the school is their battlefield. They need your constant prayer back-up. They need you to prepare their minds for war.

God has appointed parents, and indeed the Church, as platoon commanders for children. Our duty is to teach them the constitution and policy of the WORD. In Jesus name, they will win on the battle field called "school". They will win because their God is a winner!

I pray that this book has been an eye opener for you, and has re-charged your prayer batteries so that you can begin, continue and intensify prayers for your children and for children all over the world. God bless you.

If this book has blessed you and you want the author to know about it or if you want details about Grace Akanle's ministry and company, *Ancient of Days Educational Services Ltd.,* please write to:

**Rev. Grace Akanle
C/O PO Box 15022, London SE5 7ZL,
United Kingdom**

Introducing the

SATAN-PROOF
YOUR CHILDREN
CAMPAIGN

SATAN-PROOF YOUR CHILDREN CAMPAIGN

Christian parents have a God-given responsibility to train, nurture and protect their children within the parameters of the Faith. In the light of the book, *Satan-Proof Your Children,* by Rev. Grace Akanle, this task is paramount.

THE ISSUE

The educational environment today has become an easy avenue for Satan's well-organised attacks against children's moral and spiritual development. If he is not stopped in his tracks by concerned, God-fearing people, we would witness a total collapse of morals in the society at large. Children deserve conducive environments for the nurturing of their young minds in line with God's principles.

THE CAMPAIGN

The *Satan-Proof Your Children Campaign* has been launched to enforce the will of God regarding the moral and spiritual development of children. Particular emphasis is laid on the kind of education they receive – at school, Church and home. This ongoing campaign aims to achieve the following objectives:

(1) *raise* the awareness of parents about the issues facing the moral and spiritual growth of children in schools;

(2) *inspire* Christian parents and guardians to pray constantly for and be more involved in their children's healthy growth into adulthood;

(3) *provoke* the Church to invest more time and money into children educational programmes, the improvement of Sunday School and, ultimately, the establishment of Christ-centred learning throughout the nation.

THE STRATEGIES

The achievement of the aims stated above will be in phases, the first being the **Awareness Phase**—publishing abroad the societal and educational issues facing Christian children today. The primary strategy for accomplishing this is the book, **Satan-Proof Your Children**. The book is also the main tool for initiating this campaign.

The **Action Phase** will include a variety of initiatives that the awareness will prompt. Individual, corporate, local and national activities will be embarked upon as the Holy Spirit directs. We expect parents to start praying for their children in the light of the information in **Satan-Proof Your**

Children. This is part of the **Action Phase.** Church groups and organisations with a vision for children can come together and sponsor meaningful and helpful programmes that can achieve the campaign objectives.

The **Accomplishment Phase** of the campaign is the ultimate goal of this campaign—the establishment of Christ-centred learning centres in every Borough in London, throughout the British Isles, all over Europe and in all the world. To secure the faith of the coming generation, this task is inevitable.

WHAT CAN YOU DO?

Start from where you are today—with you own children (if you have any). Pray for your children and for children everywhere. Pray against the attacks of the devil against Children. Pray for Churches and organisations that work with Children. Pray for the present educational system. Pray for the next generation of believers.

Get involved with the **Satan-Proof Your Children Campaign.** Share the book, **Satan-Proof Your Children** with every parent you know. The Lord will crown your efforts with success.

- Tokunbo Emmanuel
for THE CAMPAIGN ORGANISERS

If you have any enquiries, comments, suggestions, or require further information about the *Satan-Proof Your Children Campaign,* please write to:

The Organisers
Satan-Proof Your Children Campaign
PO Box 15022, London SE5 7ZL
United Kingdom.

The *Emmanuel House* Vision:

Spreading the knowledge
of God's glory to the ends of the earth
by raising writers
and releasing classics;

Expounding the mind of God
for this present generation;

Motivating and inspiring
God's people towards
reality, purpose and destiny.